1—O.O.A.

OUTRIDER OF THE APOCALYPSE:

Life and Times of Joseph Bates

Outrider of the Apocalypse:

Life and Times of Joseph Bates

by Godfrey T. Anderson

PACIFIC PRESS PUBLISHING ASSOCIATION
Mountain View, California
Omaha, Nebraska   Oshawa, Ontario

Cover design by dale rusch

Dedicated to my wife, Idalene

Preface

Captain Bates was a rather complex person and difficult to understand in some ways. One cannot be exposed to the many facets of his life without developing an admiration for his sterling qualities of character. His role in the founding and early development of the Seventh-day Adventist Church has probably not been fully appreciated or understood. A special effort has been made in these pages to present the main features of his life against the backdrop of the kaleidoscope of nineteenth-century America.

The chief standard sources for the life of Captain Bates are his own *Autobiography*, written originally as a series of articles for the *Youth's Instructor* and published in that journal over a five-year period beginning in 1858. These articles carried the story of his life in a rather sketchy way up to about 1844. After the founding of the *Review and Herald* six years later, several hundred articles by Joseph Bates appeared in the columns of this journal until just before his death in 1872. These mainly reported his travels as an itinerant Adventist preacher.

Beyond these traditional sources I have sought information about Joseph Bates and his family in the various official public records in places where he lived, both in Massachusetts and in Michigan; in various surviving legal documents; in the records of New Bedford and Fairhaven, Massachusetts, land transactions; in material located in the Melville Whaling Room of the New Bedford free public library; in the Old Dartmouth Historical Society on Johnnycake Hill in New Bedford; in the Public Records office in Chancery Lane, London; and through personal contacts at Dartmoor Prison at Tavistock in west England. Genealogical records and vital statistics in various places helped to fill in some of the gaps in the material, particularly involving personal and family matters.

Descendants of Joseph and Prudence Bates have been located in New York, Pittsburgh, and Tulsa. They were invariably helpful in my researches, particularly in matters pertaining to his personal life. The picture of Prudence Bates which appears in this book is the only known picture we have of Joseph's wife. This is also true of the miniature painting of Joseph Bates as a young man. Both of these are published for the first time in this volume.

It would not be possible to mention specifically all those who in one way or another gave helpful assistance in the research for this sketch. Without their help, however, it would have been impossible to accomplish even the limited study that was attempted in this volume. Special mention should be made of Dr. Robert Cleveland, vice-president for academic affairs, and of Dr. J. Paul Stauffer, dean of the graduate school, both of Loma Linda University. Each gave valuable assistance and encouragement in the work of bringing this study to consummation.

I hope that this study may lead others to explore further various personalities of Adventist history and that the inspiration and contribution of the God-fearing pioneers of this reforming religious movement may become better known to the current generation.

Godfrey T. Anderson.

Loma Linda, California
January 15, 1971

Contents

1. The Habitat of a Mariner   13
   (1792-1807)

2. Britain Waives the Rules   18
   (1807-1814)

3. Violence in the Tomb of the Living   23
   (1814-1815)

4. The Acquisitive Years   29
   (1815-1827)

5. Captain Bates Lays Down the Law   34
   (1827-1828)

6. Utopia in Bloomers   40
   (1828-1839)

7. Herald of the Morning   45
   (1839-1844)

8. Lo, the Bridegroom   54
   (1844)

9. "What's the News, Captain Bates?"   61
   (1845-1849)

10. "Neither Snow, nor Rain, nor Heat,
    nor Gloom of Night"   69
    (1850-1852)

11. The Sea Rover Pitches a Tent   79
    (1853-1855)

12. Years of Transition   85
    (1856-1858)

13. Westward the Course of Adventism   90
    (1858-1860)

14. A Church Is Born   97
    (1860-1863)

15. A Health Reformer Shows the Way   104
    (1863-1868)

16. "Home Is the Sailor"   113
    (1868-1872)

Genealogical Chart   121

Map   122

Notes and References   125

Bibliography   129

Index   137

Earliest known picture of Joseph Bates, painted when he was approximately twenty-six years old. Portrait belongs to Mrs. George H. Tabor of Rye, New York.

1

THE HABITAT OF A MARINER

(1792-1807)

Seventeen ninety-two was a memorable year in the history of the New World. It was the tercentenary of the first landfall made by Christopher Columbus and his men in the Western Hemisphere. A grand celebration in America of this historic event was held in New York City on October 12, 1792. On that day also the first memorial to Columbus in the United States was dedicated in Baltimore.

It was the year construction of the national Capitol and the White House in Washington got under way. The Union admitted Kentucky. The Bill of Rights became an integral and significant part of the Constitution. George Washington, just completing his first term as President, was eager to retire to private life. John Hancock, of American Revolution fame, was Governor of Massachusetts.

Meanwhile France, and in fact all of Europe, was convulsed with revolution and its wide-ranging repercussions. The centuries-old monarchy in France was suspended in 1792, and the first French Republic was proclaimed.

Into such a world of innovation and change, on July 8, 1792, in the village of Rochester, Massachusetts, situated some seven miles from the port town of New Bedford, Joseph Bates was born. Within a year his parents moved to bustling New Bedford to spend the rest of their days in this vicinity. That portion of New Bedford east of the Acushnet River, where the Bates family lived, was set aside in 1812 under the name Fairhaven, and has continued under this name to the present.

Named after his father, Joseph was the fifth of seven children, four boys and three girls.* In his autobiography Joseph Bates sheds little light on details of his family background. His older brother, Anson, became a physician and settled in Barre, Massachusetts. The Massachusetts Medical Society confirms that he was admitted to membership in 1813, and died in 1836 at the age of forty-nine. A younger brother, Franklin, a seaman, sailed with his brother Joseph and took over his ship, the *Empress*, when Joseph retired from the sea in 1828. An older sister, Sophia Bates Bourne, was still alive in Boston in 1840, when correspondence indicates Joseph showed concern for his sister's spiritual welfare. Another sister, Harriot, two years his senior, was still living in 1868. Joseph wrote to this sister in July of that year to quell reports that he and his wife were in straitened circumstances, saying in the same letter: "I expect to see New England once more before it is lain [sic] in ruins."[1]

Joseph's father was born in Wareham, Massachusetts, in 1750. He served in the American Revolutionary War, some of the time under the celebrated French general, the Marquis de Lafayette, and rose to the rank of captain. When Lafayette visited Boston in 1825, he remembered his former companion in arms and, greeting him by name, managed to impress the elder Bates greatly.

Joseph's mother was the former Deborah Nye of Sandwich, Massachusetts.

Early in the nineteenth century, New Bedford became the whaling metropolis of the world.[2] When the Bates family moved there in 1793, its population, including Acushnet and Fairhaven, amounted to just over 3,000. In 1801, when Joseph Bates first became conscious of his surroundings, New Bedford was described as having 185 wood dwelling houses, a Quaker meetinghouse, and a Congregational church, two schools, an almshouse, a public market, three north-south streets, and twelve right-angle east-west streets.[3]

During the first half of the nineteenth century, New Bedford grew steadily, so that by the time of the Civil War it could boast more than 22,000 inhabitants. Its whaling fleet at this time numbered 330 vessels, and by 1831 Fairhaven with its separate corporate status became the third whaling center, after New Bedford and Nantucket.† The industries relating to whaling, such as cooper shops, refineries, and rope-making plants, contributed to making

---

*His father's will on file at Taunton, Massachusetts, the county seat, confirms this.
†As late as 1858, when Bates moved to Michigan, forty-eight whaling ships were sailing out of Fairhaven.

New Bedford in this period the fifth shipping port in the nation, and it was crowding Baltimore closely for fourth place.[4]

A New Bedford whaler, the *Dartmouth,* was involved in an early important action prior to the American Revolution. This ship was the first large vessel built in New Bedford. In 1773, after taking a cargo of whale oil to London, she was loaded with tea for Boston. The *Dartmouth* was one of the three ships boarded by a band of men in Indian dress, thus contributing her chests of tea to the Boston Tea Party.[5]

Some sources indicate that the majority of the citizens of New Bedford, in its early heyday as a whaling post, were Quakers. Whaling dominated all aspects of life in New Bedford. On Johnny Cake Hill stood the Whaleman's chapel, with its pulpit built to represent the prow of a ship. This was ascended, according to legend, by the minister, a former whale harpooner, by means of a rope ladder which he drew up after him. It is said that the following hymn was sung here each Sunday:

"The ribs and terrors of the whale
    Arched over me in dismal gloom,
While all God's sunlit waves rolled by
    And left me deepening down to doom.

"I saw the opening maw of hell,
    With endless pains and sorrows there;
Which none but they that feel can tell—
    Oh, I was plunging to despair.

"In black distress I called to God,
    When I could scarce believe Him mine.
He bowed His ear to mine complaints—
    No more the whale did me confine."[6]

In such a mixture of sights and sounds and smells in New Bedford, young Joseph Bates spent his early impressionable years. Under such circumstances one could hardly expect a young adventurous boy such as Joseph to be deaf to the call of the sea.

The elder Joseph Bates was public-spirited, and in 1797 his name appears as one of the founders of New Bedford Academy, which achieved a certain amount of fame as Fairhaven Academy. The sixteen founders voted $1,400 to build a structure to house the school, and the senior Joseph Bates served on a committee of two, named to purchase a lot and superintend construction. This committee was to be compensated two and a half percent on the amount for their efforts. The first year after the school was incorporated, Joseph Bates was elected treasurer for the year 1798. The academy in the early period charged two dollars a quarter for tuition. In addition to preparing young people for college it apparently very soon took children of the lower grades as well. As a school the academy had a varied existence. Sometimes there was school, sometimes not. After public schools were more abundant, it was increasingly used as a meeting hall for various purposes. The original structure still stands, but not on the original site.

It is likely that until he went to sea at age fifteen the child Joseph Bates attended this school. The following description of the interior, which is still intact, was written by a native chronicler of old Fairhaven:

"The teacher's platform was raised fully two feet above the floor, so that he could overlook every part of the room. These plain, solid, board affairs contrast strangely with the neat, slenderly built desks and seats of the modern schoolroom, but it is doubtful that any schoolroom of today can boast better scholastic work than that of the establishment of a century ago.

"At the end of each of these rooms are the same old fireplaces, which in former ages sent a merry glow of warmth and cheer over the rooms. Today they look a trifle drear, but in their day they were the most approved type. On three sides of each room are the same old windows, opening of good size, but glazed in those small panes of glass which were strictly up-to-date a century ago. The interiors of the desks disclose the fact that the boys and girls of generations past were not so very strikingly different from those of today. They left behind them many reminders of idle moments in the form of scribbled doggerel or scratched signatures and initials."[7]

Both Joseph Bates and his father participated in many land transactions during their adult lifetimes, as the records from the New Bedford records office attest. However, from the time his parents moved to New Bedford in 1793, when young Joseph was less than a year old, until he went off to sea in 1807, the family lived at Meadow Farm, which is still being used as a home known as the Darden residence, the oldest home in the community. It was from Meadow Farm that Joseph left his family to take up life at sea, and it was to Meadow Farm that Joseph returned to relate to his family and friends the many adventures he experienced at sea during his early career.[8]

It is not hard to understand the early longing Joseph felt to live the life of a seaman. All about him people and influences led him in that direction.

It was commonly said that the population of New Bedford was divided into three parts—those who were away on a voyage, those who had just returned, and those who were getting ready to embark.

Joseph's parents tried without success to dissuade him from a career at sea. Finally, in the hope that a short trip might put an end to his desires along this line, his father arranged to have him sail to Boston with his uncle. But this trip only confirmed his resolve. Thus in June, 1807, when he shipped out as a cabin boy to London via New York City, a new and highly exciting chapter in his career began. For the next twenty-one years he devoted himself to the life of a seaman, achieving in the process many exciting adventures and a reasonable degree of affluence.

2

BRITAIN WAIVES THE RULES

(1807-1814)

Joseph was fifteen years old when he sailed out of New Bedford as a cabin boy on the new ship *Fanny*. During the first year hazards to American shipping reached a high point. Although the United States and Great Britain avoided war for another five years, there was much provocation at this time. Thus young Joseph set out on the Atlantic precisely at a time when diplomatic storm signals and alarms of trouble were appearing on all sides, gravely affecting the maritime trade of the United States.

France and England warred almost continuously from 1793 until 1815. Napoleon, defeated at sea in the Battle of Trafalgar, embarked on an ambitious project of shutting English and neutral ships from ports of the Continent, thus opening what has been called the war between the elephant and the whale, each supreme in its own element. During this period a major struggle relating to the freedom of the seas emerged. The youthful American republic, which had historically reaped from time to time certain advantages from the strife of Europe, was now caught in the middle of the vast struggle between France and Great Britain. Privateers plied the seas, endangering American ships. And British ships began impressing American sailors into the British navy.

With the Anglo-French strife reaching something of a climax on the seas in 1807, young Joseph Bates faced these risks as he walked the deck of the *Fanny*. This vessel had a pleasant crossing, however, and brought its large cargo of wheat to dock at London. Although on this his first long voyage Joseph suffered from seasickness, he soon recovered. But on the return journey he was to be the main actor in high drama at sea.

He relates his experience in his *Life Sketch,* which he first wrote out without benefit of notes or diaries when he was past sixty-five. In this sketch, first appearing in the form of fifty-one articles in the *Youth's Instructor* from 1858 to 1863, he reveals a remarkably accurate memory for details. Undoubtedly this particular adventure at sea on the return trip of his first voyage made an indelible impression on his young mind.[1]

On this Sunday, almost three weeks out of England, the sailors spotted a large shark following the *Fanny.* Efforts by the crew to rid themselves of it were of no avail. Late that day the novice cabin boy, Joseph Bates, descending from the main-topgallant masthead, lost his footing and plunged unceremoniously into the sea. A rope was thrown to him, to which he was able to cling until brought to the deck of the ship. He had momentarily forgotten about the shark; but when its whereabouts were mentioned, he became greatly agitated. Apparently the shark had momentarily changed its position just about the time Joseph plunged into the sea. Had this not been the case, the story of his life would probably have come to an abrupt ending.

The lure of the sea affected many coastal New England boys and young men as it had Joseph Bates. In a number of cases the early wanderlust was cured by the first voyage, particularly if it was rough and unpleasant, but if a cabin boy remained and did his work faithfully, promotions to an officer's berth were not too long in coming. Rapid growth in tonnage of American shipping in the early days of Bates's career at sea created a large demand for officers. His own rapid ascent up the ladder to ship captain illustrates this and testifies as well to his qualities of industry and dependability. The pay for seamen was not high in this period, but it was better than that paid for most jobs on shore. A Massachusetts senator gave the average pay of American seamen at this time as $22.50 a month; but the seaman also, of course, received his quarters and board, to be added to this in arriving at a comparable figure to those working on land.[2]

The only other voyage Bates alludes to in his *Autobiography,* before his impressment in 1810, was one from New York to Archangel, Russia, which departed in the spring of 1809. In this instance his ship came near to destruction in the icebergs near the Banks of Newfoundland. This episode brought young Joseph, who was still in his teens, face to face with the real probability of death. The screams of his companions, begging God for mercy, etched vivid scenes in his memory.

Many years later he wrote his reaction to the experience: "Oh, the dreadful thought!—here to yield up my account and die, and sink with the wrecked ship to the bottom of the ocean, so far from home and friends, without the least preparation, or hope of heaven and eternal life, only to be numbered with the damned and forever banished from the presence of the Lord. It seemed that something must give way to vent my feelings of unutterable anguish!"[3]

Through a remarkable series of events, and in spite of what appears to have been an inept and cowardly captain, the vessel was released from its icy trap, and though almost disabled, was able to proceed. Two weeks later it limped into the River Shannon in Ireland. There it was repaired and refitted for the remainder of the trip to Russia. This leg of the voyage brought the ship into danger from England's enemies on the Continent and from privateers. So the ship joined a British convoy. After a storm scattered the fleet of ships, Bates's ship tried to make its way alone. However, soon two Danish privateers overtook it and brought their prize into Copenhagen.

When questioned by the judges investigating the case in Copenhagen, Joseph, the youngest and first on the stand, saved himself from losing two forefingers and a thumb by testifying truthfully about the voyage. This he did in spite of efforts by the ship's owner to have the crew give a false story which he hoped would lead to their being allowed to proceed. The judges decided that the ship and its cargo were to be confiscated, and so Joseph was able to arrange passage first to Prussia, then to Belfast, Ireland, and finally to Liverpool. Here he hoped to find passage to his homeland, but in fact more than five years were to elapse before the adventurous young seaman was to see the familiar sights of New Bedford again and the faces of his family and friends.

The British continually needed manpower to staff their fleets. The conditions which prevailed in the navy at this period (low pay, filthy and dangerous quarters, poor and meager rations, and floggings) led to many desertions. Also these conditions made it virtually impossible to recruit young men. Thus the British followed the practice of impressing men into the navy. Also, because many British deserters joined the American merchant marine or navy, Britain claimed the right to stop and search American merchant ships in quest of deserters. Because little effort was made to distinguish American seamen from British, by this means Britain forced thousands of Americans into the British navy during this period.[4] Besides this, pressgangs, in English port cities and elsewhere, actually kidnapped men to serve in the navy, and here again citizens of the United States were taken in spite of protests and legitimate documents establishing their true citizenship.

It was such a press gang—twelve men and an officer—which on an April evening in 1810 seized Joseph Bates and his companions at a boarding house in Liverpool. They were "seized and dragged" to a place of confinement. The next morning they were examined before a naval lieutenant and then forced into the British navy.

Bates was placed on board the *Princess,* of the Royal Navy, on which he said were sixty others who claimed to be Americans. Later he was transferred to a large stationary ship on which were fifteen hundred others who claimed to be in the same predicament. Eventually he, with a hundred and fifty of his compatriots, was assigned to H.M.S. *Rodney,* which carried seventy-four guns and a crew of seven hundred. His great preoccupation since being taken by the press gang was to escape. But all his efforts failed. After participating for many months in the blockade of Napoleon's ships at Toulon, H.M.S. *Rodney* was scheduled to return to England for periodic renewal.

Joseph was put aboard the *Swiftshore,* of seventy-four guns, which already carried about twenty-two Americans. About that time the United States went to war with England for several reasons, some unrelated to maritime rights. High on the list of causes, however, was the matter of impressment, a major cause of the so-called Second War for American Independence, the War of 1812.

When news of the official American entrance into the war reached Bates and his American companions, he and about six others made it clear to their superiors that they would not serve against their own country in time of war and formally requested to be considered prisoners of war. Their request was somewhat grudgingly granted, and for eight dreary months they continued aboard the *Swiftshore* as prisoners of war.

Meanwhile, Joseph's father was working through contacts with President Madison and Massachusetts Governor Brooks to effect the release of his son. As a result, contact was made just before the outbreak of the War of 1812 with the captain of the *Swiftshore;* but as time went on, it became apparent that nothing was to be done. During the first three years of his absence from home, this was the only exchange which Bates had with his family.

From the *Swiftshore,* Bates and others were sent to Gibraltar, then to an old hulk, the *Crownprinzen,* near Chatham Dock, seventy miles from London. Here with seven hundred prisoners crowded in on two decks, conflict between prisoners and authorities arose over rations. In the summer of 1814 the men were transferred again, this time to the ominous and forbidding Dartmoor Prison, "the abode of lost and forgotten men," in the region of Tavistock north of Plymouth.

Here Joseph Bates spent the last eight months of his incarceration. Since his seizure by the press-gang in Liverpool, he had spent five years to the day, under British jurisdiction, half engaged in active service in the British navy and half imprisoned, on shipboard first, and finally in the dreary granite prison on the moor.

3

VIOLENCE IN THE TOMB OF THE LIVING

(1814-1815)

In the Public Record Office in Chancery Lane in London is the original handwritten entry book used to record certain facts about prisoners of war admitted at the time of Bates's incarceration in 1814. There one finds the original longhand record of prisoner No. 3195, Joseph Bates, seaman from H.M.S. *Swiftshore,* brought over from Chatham, and received into custody at this facility on September 11, 1814. In this record he is described as twenty-one years of age, five feet nine inches, stout, visage round and sallow, with brown hair, gray eyes, and a mole on the right cheek. He was issued at this time a hammock and a blanket. The day of his discharge agrees with Bates's recollection in his *Autobiography*—April 27, 1815.[1]

Dartmoor Prison is located in the moors about fifteen miles north of Plymouth. Bates stresses the melancholy aspect of this "dreary waste." Today it is still in operation, not for prisoners of war but as a regular prison for almost six hundred of the more seasoned criminals of England. In 1814 it contained six thousand prisoners in its seven granite buildings, some of which, renovated and improved, are still in use. A central building, Bates mentions in his life sketch, housed "colored prisoners," segregated in prison No. 4 on petition of the white prisoners, most of them from New England which soon was to be known as a radical abolitionist stronghold.

Years later Captain Bates wrote out this description of Dartmoor as he knew it in 1815: "The prisons were three story, with a flight of stone steps at each end, open in the center. There was one iron-grated porthole on each

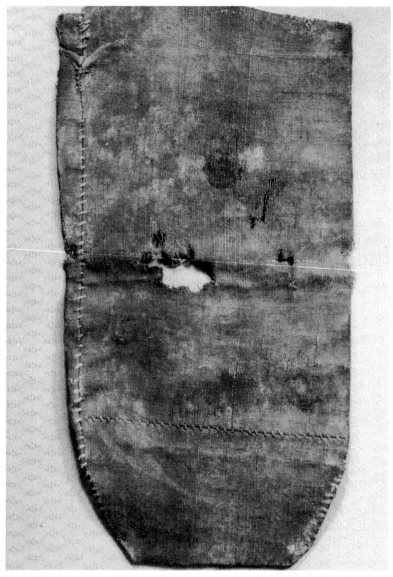

The plaque under this display reads: "Except the clothes he was wearing this bag was the sole possession of Joseph Bates of Fairhaven, Massachusetts, when at the age of 22 years on April 27, 1815, he was released from Dartmoor Prison, England, where he had been confined as a prisoner of war."

gable end. We were guarded by a barrack of six hundred soldiers, counted out in the morning, and driven in at sunset. It was quite a sight, when the sun shone, to see those who desired to keep themselves decent, seated in groups about the yard, clearing their blankets and beds from vermin."[2]

Religious meetings were conducted on Sundays in the Negro quarters. A pool in the yard served as a baptistery for converts.

From a journal compiled by Charles Andrews, a prisoner at Dartmoor from the beginning of the war to the release of all prisoners, we receive a further description of life at Dartmoor. In this journal published in 1815 Andrews wrote: "The prison at Dartmoor . . . is surrounded on all sides as far as the eye can see by the gloomy features of a black moor, uncultivated and uninhabited except by one or two miserable cottages, the tenants of which live by cutting turf on the moor and selling it at the prison. The place is deprived of everything that is pleasant or agreeable, and is productive of nothing but woe and misery. . . . On entering this depot of living death we first passed through the gates and found ourselves surrounded by two circular walls, the outer one of which is a mile in circumference and sixteen feet high. The inner wall is distant from the outer thirty feet, around which is a chain of bells suspended by a wire, so that the least touch sets every bell in motion and alarms the garrison. On the top of the inner wall is placed a guard at the distance of every twenty feet, which frustrates every attempt to escape, and instantly quells every disorderly notion of the prisoners. . . . Inside of the walls are erected large barracks, capacious enough to contain one thousand soldiers, and a hospital for the sick. This much for the courtyard of this seminary of misery; we shall next give a description of the gloomy prison itself."[3]

He explains that prisons one, two, and three were built of rough, unhewn stone, three stories high. Each of the prisons was built to contain fifteen hundred prisoners. Attached to the yard of each prison was a house of correction called a "cachot." Into this cold, dark, and damp cell the unhappy prisoner was cast if he violated the rules of the prison and remained days and even weeks on two thirds of his usual allowance of food, without hammock or bed, and nothing but a stone pavement for his chair or bed. Also to each prison was attached a small yard with a constant stream of water passing through it.

This same writer describes the weather as being constantly wet and foggy, on account of the situation of the prison, which was on a mountain, two thousand feet above the level of the sea. It was in the midst of clouds during a storm, and hence these fogs and torrents of rain. In the winter it was much colder than the country below.

Then Charles Andrews gives his first impressions upon entering Dartmoor: "We entered the prison, but here the heart of every American was appalled. Amazement struck the unhappy victim; as he cast his hopeless eyes around the prison he saw the water constantly dropping from the cold stone walls on every side, which kept the floor (made of stone) constantly wet and cold as ice. All the prison floors were either stone or cement, and each story contained one apartment, and resembled long, vacant horse stables. There were in each story six tiers of joists for prisoners to fasten their hammocks to. . . . On each side of the prison is left a vacancy for a passage from one end of it to the other. We were informed that the prisoners must be counted and massed six together every morning by the guards and turnkeys."[4]

At Dartmoor while Bates was there, there were at least fifteen prisoners from New Bedford and four from Fairhaven. These four were Joseph Bates, James O'Neil, Lemuel C. Wood, and Charles Proctor.[5]

A good share of the time the prisoners occupied themselves with making plans to escape. Bates seemed to have been among the leaders in these projects. Betrayed by one of their own number, after performing a herculean task of tunneling under the walls, the slight stream of escaping prisoners was halted before Joseph was able to make his way out. Meanwhile at Ghent on Christmas Eve, 1814, the warring nations signed the treaty ending the conflict. As weeks passed without provision for their release, the Dartmoor prisoners became restive. To express impatience with the American consul at London, Mr. Beasley, they hanged and burned him in effigy in the courtyard.

One more unfortunate and explosive event was to take place. In early April, before the men were released from the prison at Dartmoor, a series of events relating to the amount and quality of bread rations led to the so-called Dartmoor Massacre. Many of the men had experienced a confrontation of this sort while still on the *Crownprinzen,* the ship on which most of them spent time before they transferred to Dartmoor. The prisoners adamantly demanded their full ration of bread. The governor of the prison, Captain Shortland, as adamantly refused. In this tense atmosphere a trifling incident precipitated an order to fire on the prisoners. Seven Americans were killed and about sixty wounded. Joseph Bates, erstwhile cabin boy and now a man of twenty-three, witnessed at close hand the agony and confusion of the occasion.

This incident became something of a *cause celébrè* with John Quincy

Adams, who was appointed to serve on the court of inquiry. American newspapers, particularly those in New England featured prominently proceedings of the inquiry and all aspects of the incident. John Q. Adams felt the conduct of Captain Shortland was "altogether unjustifiable."[6]

The New Bedford *Mercury,* because Bates and other local citizens were there, printed a complete report of the committee's inquiries, concluding that among the Americans confined at Dartmoor were "several of genius and education" who had written songs of military and naval victory, and stating that one inmate had sold a manuscript describing the incident for nine hundred dollars.[7] In the end, the British agreed to provide some compensation for the bereaved and suffering families.

Before the end of April, 1815, the month of the massacre, Dartmoor released her prisoners. Many of those mustered before Captain Shortland and his men carried white flags on poles, with black letters saying "Massacre of American prisoners in Dartmoor prison, April 6, 1815." Or "The bloody sixth of April." These they held aloft as they made their way the fifteen miles to Plymouth and through the town to the ships that were to take them home.

As for Joseph Bates, he looked back from the heights of Dartmoor upon the bleak and dreary prison, and when he saw the western horizon for the first time in eight months, his thoughts of home and freedom almost overwhelmed him. He stooped to relatch the old pair of worn-out shoes he had on, and confidently set out on the tedious journey to Plymouth. When they reached Plymouth, he recalled, "the people stared at us; and no marvel, for I presume they had never seen so motley a company of men with such singular flags flying, pass through their city before."[8]

The final act in this six-year drama of the young sea adventurer came on the voyage home in the English merchant ship *Mary Ann* out of London. The *Mary Ann* set out for America with 280 passengers. Twice during the voyage the men took over command of the ship—once during a time of obvious danger in the ice fields off Newfoundland, and again when the port of destination was disputed. They finally brought the ship to New London, Connecticut, from where they scattered to their respective homes. The fact that their action of taking over the ship constituted mutinous conduct caused them some concern, but not enough to deter them from it.

After an absence of six years and three months, Joseph joined his family one evening in mid-June. But he did not see his father until the elder Bates returned from a business trip a few days later. For his long absence the youthful seaman had little to show save some worn garments and a canvas bag given him when he was about to escape from the *Crownprinzen* a year earlier. He had received a total of $62.71 in wages from the British agent in 1813, all he ever received from this source. In later years when he wrote his life sketch, he expressed a flair for humor rarely displayed when he said, "But if England feels disposed at this late hour of my sojourn here, to do me justice, it will be very acceptable." Prior to his move to Dartmoor, Joseph had received some financial help through an agent from his father.

Parents, brothers, and sisters warmly welcomed home the long absent one. And among them was his childhood friend, Prudence Nye, who in a few years became his wife.

Joseph Bates senior was highly pleased to find that during the long, difficult years his son had not taken up the bad habits of so many who took to strong drink to drown their troubles. Bates, however, later took up the habit, limiting himself to one glass a day. But he gave it up in 1821, after less than two years of drinking.

After the first thrill of reunion at home with his family and friends, Joseph faced the prospect of his future, and, incredible as it may seem, in spite of his many hardships and difficulties at sea, he held firm to his decision to make of the sea his career.

4

THE ACQUISITIVE YEARS

(1815-1827)

Few dates serve as a turning point in history as well as 1815. With the final downfall of Napoleon and the triumph of conservatism and legitimacy in Europe, the victors directed their attention to restoring the *status quo* as far as this could be accomplished following the turbulent years of the French Revolution and the Napoleonic aftermath.

To a degree the United States turned its back on Europe and attended to domestic issues, not the least of which related to the vast virgin continent beckoning the fit and the daring westward. Partisan politics ebbed low, a fact contributing to the myth of the so-called "Era of Good Feeling." From time to time diplomatic crises still threatened, as the announcement of the Monroe Doctrine in 1823 attests. And Jefferson's "firebell in the night" figure warning of potential troubles over slavery was dramatized in the Missouri Compromise discussions. On balance, however, during the dozen years following the War of 1812 the young American republic expanded and prospered.

The maritime trade shared in this prosperity; and now, with his experience at sea, Joseph Bates found his services in greater demand. During this twelve-year period he logged many miles at sea. His life sketch written more than forty years later devotes almost two fifths of its pages to this period. In these years he completed at least ten trips. More than three fourths of the time from 1815 to 1828 he spent away from home.

Also in this period he rose to second mate, to chief mate, and finally in

The home of Joseph Bates in Fairhaven, Massachusetts. The front porch and the garage were added since Joseph lived there.

1821, at the age of twenty-nine, to ship's captain. Before he retired from the sea in 1828 he had become part owner of his ship, and supercargo. The success of his various voyages at sea would lead to the conclusion that he had fared well financially during the years of his active maritime career and that he was in a position to retire with a reasonably comfortable living for those days (a "competency," as it was called). Most writers have estimated that this "competency" amounted to about $11,000.* At the death of his parents about this time he inherited in addition a portion of the family lands and possessions.

Joseph Bates's will, drawn up many years later, tells little about his holdings at this time. We do know that he gave all he possessed to advance the cause of Adventist evangelism after he joined William Miller in 1839. His frequent involvement in land transactions in this period reached a climax in early 1844 when he sold a major holding for $4,500.[1]

In this recital of his experiences at sea during these years he alludes to some of the things that especially impressed him at the time. On one occasion he shipped out as first mate on the brig *Francis F. Johnson* of Baltimore. The crew was, by the captain's own choice, made up entirely of black men. Of this trip Bates comments wryly, "I often regretted we were sometimes placed in peculiar circumstances in consequence of being in the minority."

When Bates returned to his New Bedford home in January, 1818, he had been away for two and a half years. In the past ten years he had been home just three times. However, this first love which he had for the sea seemed not to have discouraged his childhood friend, Prudence Nye, in her steadfast devotion to him. A month after his return home from his last journey, on Sunday evening, February 15, 1818, Joseph Bates and Prudence Nye were married by the Reverend Mr. Wheeler at Fairhaven. Although there is little to be found in the extant records about Prudence, she was an exceptionally patient and faithful wife, and a godly influence on her husband and family. Prudy, as she was called by her husband and close friends, was given to self-effacement, accepting without complaint what must have been at times a lonely and Spartan existence. Census statistics, however, suggest that she had the company of her widowed mother living at the Bates residence for forty years.

Their first child, a son, Anson Augustus, born November 15, 1819, died

---

*In recent years one writer, alluding to Bates, mentions that amount as $30,000, the sum being arrived at, very likely, with the aid of editorial license.

before his second birthday. Their second child, Helen, Joseph saw for the first time in 1824 upon his return from a voyage. She was sixteen months old at the time. The Decennial Federal Census of 1820, while not listing other than heads of family by name and age, suggests that at that time in the Bates household were Joseph and Prudence Bates, the one son, Anson, and Mrs. Bates's mother, Mrs. Obed Nye. Mr. Nye had died in France in 1796 at the age of thirty, leaving his widow and two daughters, Prudence and Sylvia.

The parents of Joseph Bates died within months of each other, Joseph Bates, Sr., preceding his wife in death on May 7, 1828, at the age of seventy-eight. His will on file at Taunton, Massachusetts, the county seat, lists items totaling $3,746 value in real estate, and $325.74 in his personal estate. The list of personal possessions includes such items as a horse collar, a plow, a "lanthorn," and a grindstone.

In his various voyages Joseph Bates encountered many fierce storms at sea. The very worst one, by his own testimony, came as his ship was attempting to return from Göteborg, Sweden, to New Bedford in the winter of 1818-19. This trip, which normally would require about six weeks, took in this instance about six months. Bates describes this storm as the "most peculiar and trying storm in all my experience; neither have I read of the likes in its nature and destruction."

The crew, in an effort to save the ship and their lives, dropped overboard forty tons of iron cargo into the sea. The captain even asked the ship's cook, the only black man on board, to pray for divine aid. Bates described the awfulness of this particular storm in some detail: "The raging elements seemed to set at defiance every living creature that moved above the surface of the sea. In all my experience I have never witnessed such portentous signs of a dreadful, devastating storm in the heavens. The sea had risen to such an awful height, it seemed sometimes that it would rush over our mastheads before our heavy-laden ship would rise to receive its towering, foaming top; and then the howling, raging wind above it, straining every stitch of sail we dared to show, would dash us headlong again into the awful gulf below."[2]

Needless to say, Bates and the entire crew received an exceptionally warm welcome at their home port upon finally reaching it; they had been given up for dead long before.

The storm helped bring Bates to ponder eternal things seriously. On this voyage, when at the captain's request the Negro cook prayed, Bates for the first time heard a prayer offered at sea for deliverance from the elements.

He believed God answered this prayer. Also upon his safe return home his wife told him of an especially fervent prayer offered by a visiting Methodist minister at this very time, and the ship's log confirmed that the storm coincided with this prayer. For whatever reasons, Joseph Bates in this period became more and more interested in religion, and in a wide variety of reforms as well.

During his last few years at sea Bates tended to spend more of his time reading the Bible and meditating on spiritual themes. Also in these years while still a seaman and subject to the boredom and monotony of such a life, and in the midst of companions who feared neither God nor man, he gave up progressively the use of tobacco in any form, hard liquor, beer and wine, and even profane language, often considered by sailors as one of their constitutional rights.

For some time Prudence had encouraged him to give up the life of the sea and to settle down with their family in Fairhaven. No doubt his wife's urging and influence were of some consequence, but it is obvious that other factors also bore importantly on his final decision.

Before he set out on his final voyage in 1827, Bates decided to become a baptized Christian. He had such strongly held theological views (on adult baptism and the nature of the Trinity, to cite two examples), that, because of the difference of opinion on certain of their teachings, he refused to join the Congregational Church of his parents, but was baptized by immersion and became a member of the Christian Church which his wife Prudence had been attending for some time.

Thus the ending of Bates's career as a seaman reflected to a degree his interest in religion and reform. The end of the former career ushered in his new concerns, which were to dominate the rest of his life.

In 1827 Joseph joined the Christian Church in Fairhaven and worshiped with his wife in this building, now used as a meeting place for the Boys' Club of America.

The Acquisitive Years · 33

5

THE CAPTAIN LAYS DOWN THE LAW

(1827-1828)

The full extent and degree of Captain Bates's religious and reform convictions are apparent in his account of his final sea voyage on the brig
Empress. The ships' registry in the Melville Whaling Museum in New Bedford carries the following facts regarding the *Empress:* It was built at Rochester in 1824; Joseph Bates, Jr., is given as the master; it had a single deck, two
masts, and a square stern; it was registered as a brig of 125 tons. After the
final voyage of Joseph Bates, his brother Franklin became the master, and
the following year the brig was sold at Saint Catherine's.[1]

Bates's narrative of his life reflects his increasing concern over religion
and his progress toward becoming a practicing Christian in all aspects of his
life. On his previous voyage he expressed dissatisfaction with reading "novels
and romances." He was influenced by a melancholy poem which he found
on the opening page of his New Testament, which had been placed on top
of his things in his trunk by his wife. He said he read this poem again and
again. It begins and closes in this way:

"Leaves have their time to fall,
    And flowers to wither at the north wind's breath,
And stars to set—but all,
    Thou hast *all* seasons for thine own, O Death!

· · · · ·

"Thou art where billows foam,
Thou art where music melts upon the air;
Thou art around us in our peaceful home,
And the world calls us forth—and Thou art there."[2]

On an earlier voyage he was deeply troubled about his personal relationship to God. As he walked the deck of his little ship, "his mind was like the troubled sea." He was even tempted to leap overboard and end his life, so deeply did he sense the anguish of his "unsaved" condition. The experience of presiding at the sea burial of one of his crew members sobered him further.

Just after this experience Bates made a covenant with God which he copied from a book, and which concluded with these words: " 'I renounce all former lords that have had dominion over me, and I consecrate to Thee all that I am and all that I have. . . . Use me, O Lord, I beseech Thee, as an instrument of Thy service, number me among Thy peculiar people. Let me be washed in the blood of Thy dear Son, to whom, with Thee, O Father, be everlasting praises ascribed, by all the millions who are thus saved by Thee. Amen.'

"Done on board the brig *Empress*, of New Bedford, at sea, October 4, 1824, in latitude 19° 50' north, and longitude 34° 50' west, bound to the Brazils. Jos. Bates, Jr."[3]

On this same voyage, when his ship was loading at St. Catherine's, Captain Bates continued his struggle for a satisfying Christian experience. On occasion he went to the woods with his Bible as his sole companion. There in the thick forest he went to climb a tree to escape the reptiles, and then having fixed himself securely, he would commune with his Maker. In this manner, he later testified, "I enjoyed most precious seasons in reading the Scriptures, singing, and praising the Lord. His precious truth seemed the joy of my soul, and yet strange as it may seem, I did not then believe my sins were forgiven; but I rejoice that I was still under conviction."

Not until his return to Fairhaven where, under the influence of religious meetings, including weekly prayer meetings held at his home, and Christian friends, did he achieve a feeling of complete or full conversion. At an "inquiry meeting" which he attended at Taunton during a revival there, he felt for the first time that he was a "converted" man. Of this experience he wrote: "From this time all doubts and darkness respecting my conversion and acceptance by God, passed away like the morning dew, and peace, like a river, for weeks and months occupied my heart and mind."

In the light of this experience which came to him in 1827, while his younger brother Franklin was on another voyage with the *Empress,* it is easier to comprehend his "sanctified arbitrariness" on his final voyage. This unique expedition was his last before he turned his attention and vast dedication to other projects.

On the morning of August 9, 1827, the *Empress* sailed from the picturesque whaling harbor of New Bedford, outbound for east coast ports of South America. She carried an assorted cargo and was under the command of Captain Joseph Bates, who was no novice at sailing a ship. For over twenty years, since he was fifteen, he had lived the life of a seaman. The crew had been recruited from Boston, and all except one were strangers to the ship's captain. A strong breeze blew the *Empress* out on the boisterous ocean for the long voyage south. As the night set in and the vessel departed from Gay Head light, Captain Bates called the crew aft on the quarterdeck for some instructions regarding the voyage.

Perhaps never before nor since has such a set of rules been outlined to a group of hardy, rough, seagoing men. First, said the captain, the members of the crew in addressing each other were to use their full first name. "Here's the name of William Jones; now let it be remembered while we are performing this voyage that we all call his name William. Here is John Robinson; call him John. Here is James Stubbs; call him James. We shall not allow any Bills or Jacks or Jims to be called here." In this way he went down the list of all their names and requested them to address one another in a respectful manner, and to call themselves by their given names.

The second rule he announced was that there was to be no swearing during the voyage. At this, one of the crewmen named William Dunn said, "I have always had that privilege, sir." "Well," said the captain, "you cannot have it here," and he quoted the third commandment to show how wicked it was to swear. William Dunn spoke up again and said, "I can't help it, sir." Then he pointed out that when he was called up in the night to reef topsails in bad weather and things didn't go just right he would swear before he would think of what he was saying. The captain said he would discipline him properly if he forgot this rule, and so Dunn gave the meek rejoinder, "I will try, sir."

A third unique rule laid down by the captain as land faded from sight was that there would be no washing or mending of clothes on Sunday. The captain said, "I have a good assortment of books and papers which you may have access to every Sunday. I shall also endeavor to instruct you that we may keep that day holy unto the Lord." They were to have every Saturday afternoon free to wash and mend their clothes. At sea and in the harbor he would expect them to appear every Sunday morning with clean clothes. Furthermore, there would be no shore leaves on Sundays.

"That's the sailor's privilege," Seaman Dunn again spoke out. "I have always had the liberty of going ashore Sundays." The captain was adamant, however, and said that Dunn and all the crew must live up to this rule also. Then he endeavored to show the crew how wrong it was to violate "God's holy day," and how much better they would enjoy themselves in reading and improving their minds than in joining in all the wickedness that sailors were in the habit of doing in foreign ports on that day.

Finally the captain said, "I want to tell you that we have no liquor or intoxicating drinks on board." He did have a bottle of brandy and one of gin in the medicine chest. These he would administer when he thought members of the crew had need of their medicinal properties. "This is all the liquor we have on board," he said with finality, "and all that I intend shall be on board during our voyage." He strictly forbade their bringing any liquor aboard when they were ashore in foreign ports.

At the close of all this, the captain knelt down and commended his ship and his men to God, "whose tender mercies are over all the works of His hands, to protect and guide us on our way over the ocean to our destined port." The following morning all but the man at the helm were invited to the cabin to join in morning prayer, and they were told that this would be the practice morning and evening. They were all urged to come and join in these sessions. On Sundays when the weather was suitable, worship was held on the quarterdeck; otherwise, in the cabin, where there was generally a reading from selected sermons and from the Bible. There was some grumbling about being deprived of shore leave on Sunday, but the captain later reported that "we enjoyed peace and quietness while they [sailors on other ships] were rioting in folly and drunkenness."

After a passage of forty-seven days, the *Empress* arrived at Paraíba on the east coast of South America. Then the vessel continued on to São Salvador (Bahia) and points south. Most of the time Bates, on his little reform ship, traded along the stretch of modern Brazil as far south as Rio Grande near the modern Uruguay boundary. He traded with a degree of peril from privateers and pirates emanating from Brazil's neighbor to the south. The chief cargoes which Bates dealt in were dry hides, rice, coffee, and farina. Farina, a type of meal, seems to have been in great demand just about this time, and Bates seems to have been quite impressed with its nutritious qualities.

After trading for several months up and down the coast of South America, and numerous high adventures, the *Empress* returned again to New York and New Bedford. Apparently the crew made a reasonably good adjustment to the stringent regulations laid down by the captain at the outset of the voyage; except William Dunn, who had to be reprimanded once or twice during the voyage for drinking on shore leave.

On arrival in New York the crew, with a single exception, chose to remain on board to discharge the cargo and to continue with the ship until they arrived in New Bedford, where the *Empress* was to proceed to fit out for another voyage. She arrived in New Bedford on the 20th of June, 1828, almost a year after having sailed under the austere regulations announced by the captain. At this time some of the men inquired about going on another voyage, but Captain Bates had decided this would be his last. And his younger brother Franklin took over, sailing the "temperance" brig *Empress,* perhaps the first of its kind, under the same principles set up by his brother for as long as it remained under his command.

A very revealing document into the inner religious struggle of Captain Bates at this time is his logbook, which is in the old Dartmouth Historical Society library on Johnny Cake Hill in New Bedford, Massachusetts. More than just a logbook, this interesting work, handwritten and over a hundred pages in length, is more the introspections of a man deeply concerned about questions of religion and his own personal relationship to God—his spiritual condition in the light of what he now believed to be the reality of a Christian experience. It gives an insight into the strong feelings on religion which Joseph Bates was experiencing at this time.

Typical of the comments which he confided to his logbook on this trip was his entry of September 28, 1827: "I know not what the Lord is preparing me for, or why I have such conflicts in my mind. . . . But I feel sometimes such a spirit within me for fear I shall be led to commit some dreadful sin for which I know I must suffer." He alludes often to his home and family and seems to feel condemned that he has been away from them so much of the time.

Another entry of this nature is the following: "I have learned . . . how to prize the privilege of being with my dear family. . . . I feel to thank God for the dear partner of all my joys and sorrows. . . . I bless Thee for the dear woman which Thou hast given me for a helpmeet."

And near the end of the voyage he wrote: "The nearer I approach my home the (more) anxious I feel to hasten the time. I make much dependence on meeting my dear family, and sometimes I hardly dare trust myself with my feelings, fearing a disappointment."[4]

The *Sailors' Magazine and Naval Journal* published by the American Seaman's Friends Society reported that forty ships sailed from New Bedford in 1830 "with supplies of distilled liquor for medicinal use only"; and then it went on later to add that seventy-five similarly equipped vessels sailed from New Bedford a year later. As a part of the reform wave of this period there was a great deal of concern expressed over the welfare of seamen, and most seamen who were acquainted with ship life seemed to agree that hard liquor was the most serious problem they had to deal with in connection with the seagoing men of the period.

Joseph Bates knew from his years as a seaman that life at sea in this period was often brutal and brutalizing. His "temperance ship" was a success, and apparently influenced other captains to follow a similar plan.

For the next dozen years, until the Millerite movement attracted his full attention and participation, Joseph Bates dealt with local affairs, such as his father's properties, civic matters, and particularly a variety of reforms, of which the air was full at this particular period in American history.

6

UTOPIA IN BLOOMERS

(1828-1839)

Joseph Bates took up his abode on land at almost the precise time when reform—writ large—became dominant in America. In Emerson's words: "In the history of the world the doctrine of reform never had such scope as at the present hour." This was a period when no institution, not even man himself, was immune from scrutiny. There was a moral fundamentalism about it, and a far-ranging scope to it that set it apart from other great reform periods of history. "It was a day of universal reform—a day when almost every man you met might draw a plan for a new society, or a new government, from his pocket; a day of infinite hope and infinite discontent."[1]

Speaking from eastern Massachusetts, the heart of this reform movement, Ralph Waldo Emerson wrote: "What a fertility of projects for the salvation of the world! One apostle thought all men should go to farming, and another that no man should buy or sell, the use of money was the cardinal evil; another that the mischief was in our diet, that we eat and drink damnation. . . . Others attacked the system of agriculture, the use of animal manures in farming, and the tyranny of man over brute nature; these abuses polluted his food. The ox must be taken from the plow and the horse from the cart, the hundred acres of the farm must be spaded, and the man must walk wherever boats and locomotives will not carry him. Even the insect world was to be defended—that had been too long neglected, and a society for the protection of ground worms, slugs, and mosquitoes was to be incorporated without delay. With these appear the adepts of homeopathy, of hydropathy, of mesmerism, of phrenology, and the wonderful theories of the Christian miracles! Others assailed various vocations, as that of the lawyer, that of the merchant, of the manufacturer, of the clergyman, of the scholar. Others attacked the institution of marriage as the fountain of social evils. Others had ordered themselves to the worrying of churches and meetings for public worship, and the fertile forms of antinomianism among the elder Puritans seemed to have their match in the plenty of the new harvest of reform."[2]

As the decades of the antebellum period wore on, the wide-ranging reform impulse tended to concentrate more and more on one evil that cried out for attention: slavery. But in 1828 when Joseph Bates left the sea, there were many evils needing reform which attracted him and his compatriots. In his case, while he was active at first in the antislavery movement, his considerable penchant toward all reforms drew him into the Millerite movement of second-advent preaching. As he lost friends in the period for his course of action, he explained finally that all the evils which the reformers were attacking would disappear with the second coming of Christ. But for the decade preceding 1840 he was active in a wide spectrum of reforms.

To the Bates household had now been added a baby girl, Eliza, born in 1824. In 1830 a fourth child, Joseph, was born, who became a whaler and was lost at sea at the age of thirty-five. A daughter Mary, who became in time Mrs. Reardon, was born in 1834, the fifth and last child of the Bates family. She with her son Willie lived with her parents in Monterey, Michigan, during the last few years of their lives.

It is easy to understand the burden Bates carried for men on shipboard. From many personal experiences he knew the evils of alcoholic beverages. Beginning the very day of his baptism he proposed organizing a temperance society. Rebuffed by the minister who had just baptized him, presumably Elder Charles Morgride of the Christian Church, Bates found support from the pastor and several members of the Congregational Church. With about a dozen supporters in 1827 they founded the Fairhaven Temperance Society made up primarily of ship captains—as far as this group knew, the first such society in America. Bates wrote: "If any temperance societies had ever been organized previous to the one at Fairhaven, we were unacquainted with the fact." Actually, the very first society founded in English America to discourage the use of intoxicating liquors dated from the year when a physician in New York State led out in the movement in 1808. Other efforts in this direction followed. "A vigorous temperance movement was inaugurated in the town [of New Bedford] in 1819, and public action taken May 26 to suppress the sale of cider and other intoxicating liquors to minors, so that their morals may not be corrupted and their future prospects blasted by habits they have acquired in their youth."

However, not until 1825 did evangelical Protestantism direct its efforts on a sustained basis against the evils of strong drink. Not until 1826, the year before Bates organized his group, did the American Temperance Society come into existence. The organized reformers began to debate whether they should seek to require total abstinence or only to restrict the use of so-called ardent spirits. Bates's society adopted a teetotaler position, as did the American Temperance Society a few years later. This rigid position for a time lost them some popularity. In time the temperance advocates moved ahead to the point of even securing prohibition legislation in several of the states. By 1834 all of the states of the union had temperance auxiliaries, and five thousand local societies claimed a million pledged signers on their rolls.

Also about this time the Cold Water Army, a children's temperance group proclaiming the superior virtues of pure, cold water over alcoholic drinks of all kinds, was organized in Fairhaven for youngsters from age four and upward. The Fairhaven Cold Water Army, in which Bates showed great interest, enrolled three hundred children.[3]

During these years Bates also devoted time and energy to another rising reform movement, the antislavery impulse. Abolitionists in the North and the "fire-eaters" in the South began to attack each other. The antislavery societies also led, in the Northeast, to organized efforts by "gentlemen of property and standing" to silence the antislavery supporters. Because of his stand, Bates alienated more of his friends.

Speaking about the feelings he held in 1832, he wrote: "I then began to feel the importance of taking a decided stand on the side of the oppressed. . . . Duty was clear that I could not be a consistent Christian if I stood on the side of the oppressor, for God was not there. Neither could I claim His promises if I stood on neutral ground. Hence my only alternative was to plead for the slave, and thus I decided."[4]

Thus in the mid-1830's Bates joined the vanguard of the efforts to organize a Fairhaven Antislavery Society, later an auxiliary to the New England Antislavery Society. Initially about forty Fairhaven citizens joined this organization. The antislavery activities of Bates and others who later embraced and preached the second coming of Christ reveal the reason the Millerite message was generally unwelcome throughout the South.

In these first years after he had given up the sea, Captain Bates helped organize another reform movement, the Fairhaven Seaman's Friends Society. This organization proposed to assist in the moral improvement of seamen. As late as 1844 it was still in existence and at that time had the equivalent of a ladies' auxiliary.

Bates, also interested in foreign missions and the spiritual needs of the "heathen," assisted in the work of the American Tract Society until he became convinced that this body took an ambivalent position on the slavery issue. His efforts to apply certain theories to the operation of his small farm, left him by his father, came to naught. Another indication of Bates's diversified interests, to deal with it gently, was his experiment in raising mulberry trees to feed silkworms which would lead to the culture of silk. This seemed to many to be a passing fad, and it was not followed out to a successful culmination. Captain Bates's plan envisioned a school for young people in which they would learn the advantages of manual labor. This entire project ended when it was learned that silk culture was something that could not become rapidly successful. The fact, however, that he had ideas and projects along these lines is of special interest when we recall how influential he was as one of the founders of the Seventh-day Adventist Church with its philosophy of Christian education, which followed along lines of teaching the virtue and dignity of labor.

Although peace societies were being formed about this same time, the available evidence does not indicate that Bates devoted much time or effort in this direction. Bates did, however, seem to hold William Lloyd Garrison, a leader in this field as well as in abolitionism, in high esteem. He also admired a fellow ship captain turned farmer who was at that time the chief advocate of a Congress of Nations. Of these efforts Bates wrote, "Moral-reform societies were multiplied in various places, as were also peace societies, having for their object the abolition of war. They proposed to settle all disputes or difficulties of importance, by reference to a Congress of Nations."[5] He seems not to have developed a great interest in this particular area of reform, nor did he devote time and attention to projects of this nature.

In the 1830's Joseph Bates was occupied, too, in various real estate transactions. An examination of the volumes of real estate transactions at the office of the Register of Deeds in New Bedford reveals scores of transactions in his name, most involving small parcels of land he sold in the two decades following 1828.[6] In 1830 he sold the residence he had inherited from his father, Meadow Farm, to his brother Franklin. For the next year or so he occupied his time in building a new dwelling and outbuildings on his farm.

At the time, with three friends, he was also engaged in building for the Christian Church the Washington Street meetinghouse (now used as a boys' club).

In 1831 Joseph Bates added tea and coffee to his list of forbidden drinks. His own feelings of well-being without them led him to this position, but he also favorably quotes Sylvester Graham on the harm of tea and coffee. The views he held at this early date on healthful living also led him to hold in great esteem Sylvester Graham's other ideas regarding whole grains and natural foods.

Here then was a reformer stripped and ready for action in the great age of reform in American history, enthusiastic for the high excitement and challenge of the period, and ready to join an array of earnest and enthusiastic reform leaders. With his flaming oratory reformed drunkard John B. Gough brought out crowds and led the fight against "the demon rum." Sylvester Graham advocated the superiority of a vegetarian diet and home-baked bread and, incurring the anger of bakers and of butchers, introduced his bread and cracker formula. Amelia Bloomer won converts to the so-called "sensible costume for females" which she popularized, almost creating riots wherever it was introduced.

Observers of the period tell of societies dedicated to persuading the so-called "weaker sex" to give up the use of tea and coffee; avoid rich cakes, pastries, and preserves; and forsake snuff and tobacco as well as wine and cordials. They speak of the prevalence of utopias and cults and such incongruities as phrenology, mesmerism, animal magnetism, patent medicine cure-alls, and the ubiquitous spittoons.

The nation was electing and reelecting Andrew Jackson, forging a party system, and debating such issues as the United States Bank, internal improvements at Federal expense, and the role of the Supreme Court.

As the people of the young and vigorous republic began to hear of the apocalyptic preaching and mathematical expounding of the Millerite preachers, Joseph Bates moved steadily toward a vigorous spiritual experience, prepared for an active role, first in the Millerite movement, and later as one of the leaders who were to found the Seventh-day Adventist Church.

7

HERALD OF THE MORNING

(1839-1844)

William Miller's teachings concerning the imminent return of Jesus Christ in 1844 influenced Joseph Bates profoundly. He first heard about the second advent as taught by Miller in 1832, but did not commit himself to this teaching until 1839, when he threw his energies and resources into support of the movement. After October, 1844, when many others were disillusioned and abandoned the whole idea, Bates remained firm. He always seemed fascinated by the time prophecies, and it was not until some years after the great disappointment of 1844 that he gave up the idea of setting a particular date for the return of Christ.

Miller, ten years older than Bates and "an upright and honest-hearted farmer," became the leading advocate of the teaching of the literal return of Jesus Christ to the earth in the mid-1840's.

"What Miller added to the traditional fire-and-brimstone mixture," writes one secular historian, "was the ingredient of mathematical computation as an 'infallible' method of unraveling mysterious prophecies. This appealed strongly to Yankee ingenuity, and challenged the competitive spirit of thousands of amateur Bible-interpreters. In addition, he laid great stress upon the imminent casting down of the mighty, the wealthy, and the educated from their exalted seats, and the raising up of the weak and humble and faithful to replace them. More than that, in an age of competing utopias, when reformers were sprouting everywhere and promising everything, . . . Miller outbid them all."[1]

The time factor in predicting the coming of the cataclysmic event fascinated both Miller and Bates. Ignoring the message of other ministers who stressed the text, "Of that day and hour knoweth no man," Miller eventually set a time, which though reset on several occasions, was finally specified as October 22, 1844.

Soon after Miller began publicly preaching the second advent, an event occurred which gave credence to his message. On the morning of November 13, 1833, meteorites gave a spectacular display of "falling stars" visible throughout most of North America. This event confirmed Miller in his views of the imminent second advent as well as the accuracy of the Biblical prophecies and signs of this climactic event.

Although William Miller began his public preaching at the beginning of the 1830's, it was not until the fall of 1839 that Bates, at the invitation of a friend, attended five lectures on the second coming given at the North Christian meetinghouse in New Bedford. Some years before, he had heard about William Miller and his prediction that the Lord would come sometime soon. The lectures in New Bedford so interested and impressed Bates that he secured and studied Miller's book of nineteen lectures.

As Bates read these lectures, especially those on Daniel's prophetic time periods, his interest grew until he began actively promoting the Millerite cause. Soon (in 1840) Joshua V. Himes, a longtime acquaintance of Joseph Bates, began publishing *The Signs of the Times,* a second-advent periodical, in Boston. Himes had lived in New Bedford for a time after 1822, and the two had worked together on temperance and antislavery matters.

The Signs of the Times issues of September 1 and 15, 1840, contained a call for a general conference on the topic of the soon coming of Christ. So decidedly had Bates joined the Millerites that he was one of the sixteen signers of the call, and, with Himes and Josiah Litch, he served on the committee on arrangements.

The call for this meeting read as follows: "The undersigned, believers in the second coming and kingdom of the Messiah at hand, cordially unite in a call for a General Conference of our brethren of the United States, and elsewhere, who are also looking for the advent near, to meet at Boston, Mass., Wednesday, October 14, 1840, at ten o'clock a.m., to continue two days, or as long as then may be found best. The object of the Conference will not be to form a new organization in the faith of Christ, nor to assail others of our brethren who differ with us in regard to the period and manner of the advent, but to discuss the whole subject faithfully and fairly, in the exercise of that spirit of Christ, in which it will be safe to meet Him immediately at the judgment seat."[2]

Joseph and Prudence Bates attended this two-day session, which ended with the sending out of a pamphlet containing the lectures given at the conference and reports of the meeting. From March 13 to 19, 1841, Miller lectured in Fairhaven, largely through the efforts and planning of Joseph Bates. The meetings were well attended, about fifteen hundred coming from New Bedford, including "a large portion of the aristocracy and ministers." Four regional second advent conferences were held in 1841. Bates served as vice-president of the one which met for three days at Lowell, Massachusetts, in mid-June of that year. All these developments lifted the spirits of Joseph Bates to a high level. He wrote: "The Advent ship was making such rapid onward progress under her cloud of well-trimmed sails, that all the opposition of currents and adverse winds could not check her career."

The second major conference on the second advent, held at Boston in May of 1842, took several far-reaching actions. Bates chaired that conference.

One action approved the adoption of the prophetic chart presented by Charles Fitch and Apollos Hale of Haverhill and authorized the printing of three hundred lithographed copies. This became the much-used " '43 chart." It illustrated the prophecies of Daniel and the Revelation. It contributed greatly to the effectiveness and clarity of the presentations of the advent preachers.

In its second major action this body approved holding summer camp meetings to advance the preaching ministry. Actually, thirty-one were held in 1842, forty in 1843, and fifty-four in the crucial year of 1844.[3] The first of these was held in Canada East. While no accurate head count of attendance exists, it was estimated that five hundred thousand attended the series of camp meetings over the three-year period.

Camp meetings figured prominently in Bates's life and ministry. Early camp meetings have often been presented in an unfavorable light by students of our earlier rural institutions. No doubt some evidence of emotional excesses exist; however, an inaccurate stereotype should not be accepted.

A writer of the Boston *Post* remarked favorably on the first Millerite camp meeting. He stated: "The second advent camp meeting, which commenced at East Kingston, N.H., on Tuesday, June 29, and continued from day to day until Tuesday noon, July 5, was attended by an immense concourse of people, variously estimated at from seven to ten thousand. . . .

"The meeting was conducted with great regularity and good order from beginning to end. The ladies were seated on one side, and the gentlemen on the other, of the speaker; meals were served uniformly and punctually at the times appointed, and the same punctuality was observed as to the hours appointed for the services.

"The preachers were twelve or fifteen. Mr. Miller gave the only regular course of lectures, the others speaking occasionally. Many of the people, without doubt, assembled from motives of curiosity merely; but the great body of them, from their solemn looks and close attention to the subject, were evidently motivated by higher and more important motives. Each tent was under the supervision of a tent master, who was responsible for the good order within the same. . . . The meeting broke up with harmony and good feeling."[4]

Also, recent students of American religious history in the nineteenth century have presented a picture which differs markedly from the comments of earlier and less informed writers. One writes as follows:

"When meeting time came, the arriving worshipers in their wagons were efficiently taken in charge, told where to park their vehicles and pasture their teams, and given a spot for their tents. Orderly rows of these tents surrounded a preaching area equipped with sturdy benches and preaching stands. . . . Tight scheduling kept the worship moving according to plan. . . . Years of experience tightened the schedules, and camp-meeting manuals embodied the fruits of practice. . . . Things took on a generally homelike look. There were Methodist ladies who did not hesitate to bring their best featherbeds to spread in the tents, and meals tended to be planned and ample affairs.

"There were new rules to cope with disorderliness as well. Candles, lamps, torches fixed to trees, kept the area well lit and discouraged young converts from amorous ways. Guards patrolled the circumference of the camp, and heroic, if sometimes losing, battles were fought to keep whiskey out."[5]

The first camp meeting attended by Joseph Bates was held at Littleton, Massachusetts, in August, 1842. He became very much interested in the layout of the camp and in the presentations of the prophecies which stressed the second advent. Even a mob which invaded the camp became docile when it understood the nature and purpose of the meeting. The following month a similar encampment set up in Taunton continued for a week, with Josiah Litch as the main speaker. The preaching, the prayers, the advent hymns, all made a vast impression on Bates. Someone estimated that ten thousand were on the grounds on Sunday at Taunton. A month later Bates attended another camp meeting near Salem, Massachusetts.

Here is his description of the approach to this camp from the city of Salem: "The main streets, cross roads, lanes, and paths, seemed almost utterly jammed and crowded with teams and carriages loaded with people, beside the jam of foot passengers—all crowding through the thick, smothering dust, to the campground. Here in the large stone-wall pasture ground, interspersed with high, ragged rocks, clumps of bushes and straggling trees, bounded by woods on two sides and water on another, the city of Salem in the distance in another direction, were pitched the numerous tents for the great meeting. The big tent loomed above them all like a light-house, pointing to the looked-for harbor of the mariner, inviting the pressing multitude to enter and listen to the messengers of God proclaiming with stentorian voices the second coming of our Lord Jesus Christ."[6]

Elders Himes, Litch, Fitch, and others preached; others met with groups gathered out of doors and explained the prophetic timetable using the " '43 charts," which they fastened to the trees. Other groups of men and women passed on their way to the water to be baptized. An estimated fifteen thousand attended the Salem camp meeting on Sunday. Meanwhile second advent publications multiplied and spread into all twenty-six states of the Union and into Canada. Beyond this, concerned people sent these publications to the sparsely settled West, also to Europe, Asia, and Africa. Joseph Bates and his fellow believers felt thrilled and energized as they witnessed what appeared to them to be the greatest spiritual revival of the people since Christ's first advent. They pondered often the figure of an angel flying in the midst of heaven, saying, "Fear God, and give glory to Him; for the hour of His judgment is come."

When Bates found himself caught up so fully in the advent movement, he soon discovered that his and other churches had cooled to members believing in Miller's message. This led Bates, after some soul searching, to withdraw his membership from the Christian Church in Fairhaven and to dispose of his interest in the premises. The local chronicler of old Fairhaven reports that thirty-three members withdrew from the Christian Church and formed their own Millerite group about this time.[7]

Captain Bates had always given himself thoroughly to what he believed. He embraced the challenging concept of the second advent of Christ with utter devotion, utter sacrifice, and utter effort. He gave all his considerable material possessions to further the work. When he retired from the sea, Joseph Bates had around $12,000, a modest fortune in those days. He also shared in the estate of his parents who died about the time of his retirement

Herald of the Morning · 49

from the sea. Whatever the amount, Joseph Bates demonstrated his implicit faith in the second advent expectation in 1843-1844 by giving the entire amount to proclaim the message to the world. He was to live out the rest of his life as a witness for God, guided only by his motto, which often troubled his cautious and prudent wife, Prudence—"The Lord will provide." And He did.

Another indication of his fervor in advancing the advent message can be glimpsed in a letter which he wrote to his older sister Sophia Bourne of Boston about this time. This letter, dated at Fairhaven, December 24, 1840, pleaded with Sophia to prepare for Christ's imminent coming: "My anxiety for your complete salvation prompts me to give you the light which I fully believe God by His Spirit and Word has imparted to my mind within a few weeks, taking history for the proof of the fulfillment of prophecy. . . . I believe the 15th of February next, Christ will come, and raise the righteous dead and change the righteous living. They together will be caught up to meet their coming Lord. . . . O glory to God for such precious promises. O, say you, I can't believe it. Joseph must be crazy. I feel and believe that I am coming to my senses. O what a tremendous hour this will be to the wicked. Let us see to it, my dear sister, that we are prepared for that eventful hour. . . . This light to me is clear and conclusive and I utter and declare it without fear of contradiction or condemnation."[8] Then he indicates that Prudy joins him in these sentiments, "She says, prepare for that day, for it will soon be upon us."

But Joseph Bates did more than contribute means and write letters to his relatives and friends on the subject of Christ's second advent. In 1844 he sold his home and most of the real estate he owned and paid off all his debts. The New Bedford office of the Register of Deeds reveals a sale of Bates's property on Mulberry Street to Nash Spooner for $4,500. This instrument is dated February 6, 1844. Then he set out with H. S. Gurney of Memphis, Michigan, to take the advent message into the South. Gurney was a large, sturdy blacksmith who loved to sing gospel songs. He got in his voice practice at the forge to the beat of hammer on anvil. Years later he returned to Michigan and associated with another blacksmith, Dan Palmer of Jackson, Michigan, Bates's first convert to the Sabbath in Michigan.

This trip to the South held the risk of real danger, because most advent preachers were identified as abolitionists. Feeling on this subject was running high. H. S. Gurney, who led out in the singing, was as fearless as Bates in facing opposition and the threat of physical harm. Their hearers, particularly

Joseph attended school in this building, originally New Bedford Academy, but known to Joseph as Fairhaven Academy, from about 1800 until he went to sea in 1807.

the slaves, enjoyed hearing Mr. Gurney sing, "I'm a pilgrim, and I'm a stranger." The advent pair did not penetrate the deep South, but they did work in Maryland on Kent Island, where Bates had been cast away many years before in a storm. In spite of the difficulties they encountered, they created wherever they traveled a great interest in the second coming of Christ. Their undaunted courage saw them through many potentially dangerous situations.

Bates's courage stood him in good stead at a meeting on Kent Island when an opposer threatened to ride Bates and Gurney out of town on a rail. On this occasion the sea captain turned advent preacher replied: "You must not think that we have come six hundred miles through the ice and snow, at our own expense, to give you the Midnight Cry, without first sitting down and counting the cost. And now, if the Lord has no more for us to do, we had as lief lie at the bottom of the Chesapeake Bay as anywhere else until the Lord comes. But if He has any more work for us to do, you can't touch us!"[9] And before the meeting was over, the opposer shook hands agreeably with Bates.

That Joseph Bates maintained a sense of perspective, if not a sense of humor, is seen from an incident he records as having taken place near the town of Chester, Maryland. He says: "We were walking just before we came to the village, and met a man on foot, seemingly in great haste, who stopped and inquired if we were the two Millerites who were going to preach in that place! We answered in the affirmative. 'Well,' said he, 'I have traveled thirteen miles this morning to see you!' As he stood gazing on us, I said, 'How do we look?' Said he, 'You look like other men.'" Then, Bates says, "his curiosity being gratified, we passed on and saw him no more."[10]

As an indication of the deep impression made upon the people to whom Bates and Gurney preached on this trip, there was one meeting where at its close the people sang a hymn and were dismissed, but made no move to leave. After they were further exhorted, the same took place again—the hymn, the dismissal—but still they remained. Finally after a third formal dismissal the people slowly left the meeting.

After holding their final meeting in Elkton, Maryland, the evangelistic team made its way north, but not without presenting charts and ideas to people on the boat and on the train until they reached Boston. A little later they preached the advent doctrine on Nantucket, Martha's Vineyard, and Block Island, finding many who believed the message and joined the advent people.

Near the spring of 1844, as the time for the end of the prophetic period and the expected appearance of Christ approached, excitement increased. "Probably," wrote Bates later, "nothing since the Flood, in the days of Noah, has ever equaled it." When spring passed and Christ didn't come and time moved on into summer, perplexity was great and widespread. Now in the "tarrying time" a search was begun in the Scriptures to correct the miscalculation which had led to this early disappointment. The *Advent Shield* defended the earnestness and integrity of the leaders of the movement. Of them it wrote: "No cause of a moral or religious character probably ever made so rapid advances as the cause of Adventism. Its votaries have usually been the humble, pious, devoted members of the different churches. . . . Never have a set of men labored more faithfully and zealously in the cause of God, or with more pure motives."

So during the summer of 1844 further intensive study of the prophecies took place, and a correction in the timing projected the great day of the Lord to October 22, 1844.

But only after this further disappointment did the nature of the event to take place on October 22 become clear. Thousands of the Millerites gave up their belief. Deeply disappointed and perplexed as Joseph Bates was with the failure of Christ's coming early in 1844, he, with other sincere believers, kept the faith and persevered in his Christian witness.

8

LO, THE BRIDEGROOM

(1844)

In the 1840's the United States experienced new economic growth and development. With these changes came also new political alignments. The infant railroad grew and pushed everywhere while its older partner, the steamboat, pioneered on Western waters and off coastal shores. The Conestoga wagon, forerunner of the western canvas-covered prairie schooner, struggled through the Allegheny mountain passes. And the Erie Canal, finished and opened in 1825, carried an increasing burden of freight and passengers. The cotton gin in the South and the McCormick reaper in the North and West changed the face of agricultural industry. The candle gave way to the smoky lamp burning "devil's oil," and iron stoves proved their superior economic worth compared to the fireplace. Photographic daguerreotypes made portrait work inexpensive and more faithfully recorded memorable scenes.

At such a propitious time, the first major disappointment to the advent believers came when April of 1844 passed without the fulfillment of their hopes. Reactions varied with individuals, but there was still a large number who now identified this period as the "tarrying" or "waiting" time. They found assurance in the prophecy of Habakkuk, chapter 2, verse 3: "For the vision is yet for an appointed time, but at the end it shall speak, and not lie: though it tarry, wait for it; because it will surely come, it will not tarry."

Joseph Bates attended a camp meeting at Exeter, New Hampshire, August 12 to 17, expecting to receive new light on the questions troubling the minds of most advent believers. On the third day of the meeting Bates himself spoke at the morning service. The second coming, he insisted, was imminent, even though at the moment they were perplexed by the state of events. His message, however, lacked the necessary spark of certainty and conviction. "May the Lord help us to obtain our true position on this stormy sea," he was saying, "and again spread all our sails for the gale that shall waft us into the harbor of glory."

At this point a Mrs. Couch arose and addressed the speaker. "It is too late, Brother Bates," she said. "It is too late to spend our time about these truths, with which we are familiar. . . . It is too late, brethren, to spend precious time as we have since the camp meeting commenced. Time is short. The Lord has servants here who have meat in due season for His household. Let them speak, and let the people hear them. 'Behold, the Bridegroom cometh; go ye out to meet Him.'" She was the sister of Samuel S. Snow, who had just arrived by horseback, and who had mentioned to his sister and her husband, Elder Couch, that he did indeed have new light on this perplexing question. Bates was not taken aback or humiliated by these frank comments. But with his typical godly meekness and grace he invited Samuel S. Snow to come forward and present his views.

This Snow did, continuing on the next day, when he preached on the midnight cry. Many, including Bates, supported this "new light" presented, and as Bates later expressed it, when the meeting closed the granite hills of New Hampshire rang out with a cry, "Behold, the Bridegroom cometh; go ye out to meet Him."[1]

Upon his return to Fairhaven, Bates preached the midnight cry message with great fervor in New Bedford and elsewhere. A new awakening took place. Earlier opposition to the new views was swept away. Now the advent believers used their strength and energy to proclaim their belief in the imminent appearance of the "Bridegroom" and the end of all things earthly. Joseph Bates actively involved himself among the group of watchers, who once again brought out the great tent, purchased in 1842, with a seating capacity of between three and four thousand, and renewed their efforts to warn the world.

Those who truly and devoutly believed in the validity of October 22 as the date for Christ's coming made every preparation to meet Him at that time. Farmers who had planted crops in the spring showed their faith by refusing to harvest them. Some store owners apparently set a day upon which to give away all their stock to any who wished to come and receive it. In one store window appeared a sign reading, "This store is closed in honor of the

King of kings, who will appear about the twentieth of October. Get ready, friends, to crown Him Lord of all." The two main advent papers, *The Advent Herald* and the *Midnight Cry,* put out last editions. The *Midnight Cry* phrased its editorial in the words of Paul, "Finally, brethren, farewell. Be perfect, be of good comfort, be of one mind. Live in peace; and the God of love and peace shall be with you." The *Advent Herald* carried a message from Himes. "As the date of the present number of the *Herald* is our last date of publication before the tenth day of the seventh month," he wrote, "we shall make no provision for issuing the paper for the week following. We feel called upon to suspend our labors and await the result."

Many other events crowded the year 1844 in the United States. In a hectic presidential campaign in national politics, the two aspirants Polk and Clay vied for votes. Harrison, President for just a month in 1841, had died in office and thus brought Tyler to the office of Chief Executive. Now near the end of Tyler's term in 1844, the hustings resounded with the screaming speeches, the torchlight parades, and the tub-thumping political songs of the contesting partisans of Polk and Clay. "All of Oregon, or none," resounded on the air. After the election, the slogan "Fifty-four forty or fight" rallied the expansionists. Various issues confronted the nation: Should Texas be admitted? Should Mexico be fought? Should the Oregon country be given up to the British, or should it all be claimed up to the Russian line? All clamored for public attention in competition with the warning that the Lord could be expected to come at any time during the year. In an atmosphere such as this, the message of William Miller and his followers does not seem as unique and peculiar as it might to a later, more sophisticated generation.

In May, 1844, the new telegraph sent its first jubilant message from Washington to Baltimore—"What hath God wrought!"—and returned the more earthy tidings to Washington from the Democratic convention—"Polk nominated for the Presidency." During this eventful year Karl Marx met Friedrich Engels in Paris, and out of their friendship and collaboration came the Communist Manifesto, the basic scripture of international Communism. During this year Horace Mann returned from his European honeymoon, spent in studying schools there, and reported that education in England and on the Continent was vastly superior to that given in American public schools. In the resulting furor over his conclusions, steps were taken to improve greatly our public school system. And during this same year a mob murdered Joseph Smith and his brother Hiram, leaders of the Mormon Church, at Carthage, Illinois.

On October 22 in the more populous cities of the East, a large circus, the American Olympiad, instituted for "the advancement of refined, equestrian, and gymnastic exercises," entertained people. John B. Gough continued his dramatic lectures on the evils of intemperance. Dr. Glidden lectured on Egyptian antiquities. Ole Bull enchanted audiences with his violin. And the Swiss Bell Ringers gave concerts. Also on October 22 the Protestant Episcopal Church, concerned with such items as a mission station in Turkey and a bishopric in China, but not with the second advent of Christ, without so much as a nod to the waiting advent believers, closed its annual convention in Philadelphia.

On Sunday, October 20, in the Second Presbyterian Church in Philadelphia, a Reverend Rood preached on Matthew 24:23-27, pointing out the signs of Christ's coming and the end of the world, basing his sermon specifically on Christ's words, "Of that day and hour knoweth no man, no, not the angels of heaven, but My Father only." This minister gravely concluded that every failure of a time prediction of the end of the world produced more scoffers and infidels and did more harm than good.

While these and other significant events were transpiring in the world about them, the advent believers were quickly settling their earthly affairs. Those who had money brought it to the leaders, begging them to use it in the final warning of the world. Those in debt came asking funds with which to settle accounts, that they might not be found owing any man when Christ came. The treasurer took in what was given him, and gave out to those in need. But because of the volume of business and the haste with which it had to be transacted, he was unable to keep accounts of the amounts disbursed.

Just before October 22, the Millerite preachers returned to their homes to wait. The great tent was furled. The presses ceased to print the advent papers. Then dawned the fateful morning of October 22, 1844.

Across most of the northeastern part of the United States, the sun rose clear and bright on that crisp Tuesday, October 22, 1844. To many it was only another beautiful day. But to thousands of others, except for the day Christ rose from his little rock tomb outside Jerusalem, it was the most important day in the history of the world, a day on which prophecy had laid its finger almost twenty-five centuries before.

October 22 found William Miller in his home in Low Hampton, New York, where he had gone to rest upon completion of the work of warning the country of Christ's imminent return. Father Miller had steered clear, generally, of setting a specific day for Christ's return, and he did not agree to stipulate October 22 until just shortly before that day. He finally agreed that this was the day according to prophecy and began to preach it. Here at Low Hampton, Joshua V. Himes came to spend the day and greet the Lord with Miller, his old friend and fellow laborer.

Perhaps the day brought to Miller and Himes a deeper disappointment than to any of the others, for they had been so intimately bound up in all phases of the advent movement. Yet, confused and disappointed, Miller was not ready to disavow his faith. "Were I to live my life over again with the same evidence that I then had," he wrote, "to be honest with God and men, I should have to do as I have done. One thing I do know, I have preached nothing but what I believe; and God has been with me; His power has been manifested in the work, and much good has been effected."

William Miller remained at his farm after the disappointment. He continued to study but within three years lost his eyesight, and for the last two years of his life he remained blind. He died in 1849. His published testimony, written during those last years of his life, affirmed his belief in the validity of his experience and his continuing belief that the second coming of Christ was near at hand. Joshua V. Himes lived to be an old man. However, he chose not to continue with the Adventist group, but devoted his later years to the ministry in the Episcopal Church. To the end of his life, however, he defended the Millerite movement from those who would ridicule or belittle it as fanatical.

The advent believers saw midnight come and go. They waited for the hours to creep along till morning, and their disappointment then became a certainty. Hiram Edson, who was later to become a leader of the Seventh-day Adventist Church, wrote of this hour, which he spent at Fort Gibson in western New York, "Our fondest hopes and expectations were blasted, and such a spirit of weeping came over us as I never experienced before. It seemed that the loss of all earthly friends could have been no comparison. We wept and wept till the day dawned."

In Portland, Maine, a young girl of sixteen, Ellen G. Harmon, waited on this day with her family. She and her sisters had worked for months at their home helping their father in his hat-making trade, and knitting stockings at twenty-five cents a pair, to raise a little money they could invest in literature to warn the world of its peril. A young man, James White, who was visiting and ministering in Portland that summer, met Ellen and was impressed by her piety and zeal.

Expecting the coming of the Lord in just a few weeks, neither of them gave a thought to personal plans beyond October. Yet two years later, under different conditions and expectations, they met again and were married. The Harmon family felt the disappointment keenly, as did the other believers, and yet Ellen could later look back and write, "1844 was the happiest year of my life."

Joseph Bates spent October 22, 1844, at his home in Fairhaven with his wife and his youngest daughter, Mary, and probably Eliza, who didn't marry until 1858. His oldest daughter, Helen, had married the previous autumn. Records in the Melville Whaling Room of the New Bedford Public Library indicate that Bates's son sailed on a whaler, the *Marcus,* on October 21, 1844, at fourteen, a year younger than was his father when he first went off to sea.

After the great disappointment, Joseph Bates said, "The effect of this disappointment can be realized only by those who experienced it."[2] The morning following he went out to get some provisions for the family. Children followed him and mocked. Men pointed the finger of scorn. Years later he told a fellow Adventist preacher he had wished the earth might swallow him up, so humiliating was the experience. "You can have no idea of the feeling that seized me. I had been a respected citizen, and had with much confidence exhorted the people to be ready for the expected change. With these taunts thrown at me, if the earth could have opened and swallowed me up, it would have been sweetness compared to the distress I felt."[3]

He had given everything to the cause save for a few coins he had remaining. He had a small field of potatoes which a neighbor had wished to purchase. To him he said, "No; it would not be right to sell them to you when I know you will not receive benefit from them. Let them remain in the ground as a witness of my faith in the Master's immediate return to the earth."[4]

As might be expected, confusion and perplexity followed this great disappointment. In the spring of 1845 Adventist leaders convened at Albany, New York, in a mutual conference to decide what steps, if any, should be taken to bring order back into the movement. They felt a need for a new basis on which to regroup. Confidence was expressed at this meeting in William Miller, but several prominent former leaders were absent from Albany, including Joseph Bates.[5]

That portion of disappointed Adventists who felt strongly that the time element was correct and that the event needed further study, now went back to the Bible to study further that part of the 2300-days time prophecy. Bates joined this group.

It soon became apparent to them that they had erred in believing that the sanctuary was the earth. The prophecy, they concluded, referred to the symbolic cleansing of the heavenly sanctuary, or the beginning of the investigative judgment. Also to this group the three angels' messages now took on new meaning; and before long, light on the seventh-day Sabbath completed to their satisfaction the figure of the three angels used by John the revelator in describing their very movement and this period in religious history.

Not all of the disappointed continued with the movement. Most rejoined their former churches, mainly Methodist, Baptist, Presbyterian, and other Protestant churches. One group joined the Shakers. Some became atheists. Those who did not retreat to other religious organizations but continued to study independently, formed groups with divergent views on a variety of subjects—dividing over the nature of man's soul, eternal punishments, infant baptism, sanctification and perfection, and eventually the seventh-day Sabbath.

About this time inspired guidance came to the struggling group represented by Joseph Bates, in the form of messages which came to Ellen Harmon, now only seventeen years of age. She brought counsel which unified and directed the believers and helped to clarify difficult issues. In a providential sequence of events, the perception of the seventh-day Sabbath, center and heart of the law of God, now was introduced to the Adventists. Many embraced these teachings and upon organization into a denomination in 1863 combined this Biblical truth with that of the advent in forming the name Seventh-day Adventist.

Some still inclined to set a specific date for Christ's return, even after the disappointments of spring and fall, 1844. Joseph Bates tended to do this himself. By some logic he interpreted the wave sheaf which was waved seven times by the priest as meaning seven years, which he proceeded to add to 1844, thus coming up with 1851 as a new date for Christ to come. Ellen White, many years his junior, cautioned Bates to deal no longer with specific dates, that truly the Bible meant what it said, "Of that day and hour knoweth no man."

Because of the strategic role played by Joseph Bates in the adoption of the seventh-day Sabbath by a large segment of disappointed Adventists, this period of his life also demands special attention, including his role in disseminating this teaching. The basic church doctrines forged in these difficult times have now stood the test of a century and more.

9

"WHAT'S THE NEWS, CAPTAIN BATES?"

(1845-1849)

Following the dashing of their hopes with the passing of October 22, 1844, without the second advent, three main groups emerged. These differed on many points but still merited the title "Adventists."

The most numerous group met in Albany, New York, in April, 1845, and included Miller himself, Himes, Litch, and Bliss (later, William Miller's biographer).

The least numerous group held that the millennium had begun on the twenty-second of October. This group tended toward censoriousness and fanaticism.

Neither of these two groups accepted the seventh-day Sabbath teaching.

Numbering somewhere between these two groups were those Adventists led by Joseph Bates, James White, Ellen Harmon, Hiram Edson, and others. After they embraced the seventh-day doctrine, they were known for several years as "the Sabbath and shut-door people." This group became the nucleus of the Seventh-day Adventist Church. They used the name Seventh-day Adventist in 1850, but it was thirteen years later, and after much debate, that this became the official church designation.

Shortly before the disappointment of 1844 the question of observing the seventh-day Sabbath was getting attention in various quarters. Several references on the subject in the *Midnight Cry* indicate that these Adventists felt that there was no obligation upon the Christian to observe the seventh-day Sabbath. Some attention was given at the Albany conference of April, 1845, to "Jewish commandments and fables of men." Under this heading they apparently considered and disposed of the seventh-day Sabbath teaching.[1]

As has been indicated earlier, Bates did not attend the conference at Albany. Just a few weeks before, he had begun to observe the seventh-day Sabbath. In this he was influenced first by an article by T. M. Preble in *The Hope of Israel,* which came to Bates's attention in March, 1845. Although Preble repudiated his own faith in the Sabbath within two years, Joseph Bates read the article, embraced the seventh-day Sabbath, proclaimed it, and rejoiced in it until his death thirty-seven years later. Many months passed before Bates was joined in this by other Adventist leaders, but he never flinched from standing alone. Even his wife, Prudence, did not accept the Sabbath until 1850.

In August, 1846, Joseph Bates printed for distribution a forty-eight page tract on the subject entitled, "The Seventh-day Sabbath a Perpetual Sign, From the Beginning to the Entering Into the Gates of the Holy City, According to the Commandment." He devoted his tract strictly to the Biblical reasons for Sabbath observance, but in it Bates indicates the resolute manner in which he met and settled many issues in his eventful life.

Speaking of this decision to observe the Sabbath which he made with dispatch, he wrote in this tract: "Many things had troubled my mind as to how I could make this great change, family, friends and brethren, . . . but this one passage of Scripture was, and always will be, as clear as a sunbeam. 'What is that to thee: follow thou Me.' In a few days my mind was made up to begin to keep the fourth commandment. . . . Contrary views did, after a little, shake my position some; but I feel now that there is no argument or sophistry that can becloud my mind again this side of the gates of the Holy City."[2]

Only 250 of these Sabbath tracts were printed; but the following January, Bates printed a second edition of his tract, expanded to sixty-two pages. Explaining that the increasing demand was one reason for the second edition, he appealed for financial support for distribution of the tracts, as they were sent out without charge. In the second edition, Bates added a fuller and more complete prophetic presentation based on Revelation 14 and touched on the concept that the change of the Sabbath to Sunday is the "mark of the beast."

Hearing of Sabbath keepers in northern New Hampshire, Bates with characteristic directness traveled there and presented himself at the door of Frederick Wheeler after the family had retired. After spending the night in study and discussion of the topic at issue, the two men proceeded to Washington, New Hampshire, not very far away, and met with Hiram Farnsworth and possibly others in what has been called the first Seventh-day Adventist conference. This meeting was held under some maple trees on the Farnsworth farm. By noon, according to most reports, Bates started out for Fairhaven. At the end of his journey, on crossing the wooden bridge over the Acushnet River between New Bedford and Fairhaven, a neighbor, James Madison Monroe Hall, greeted him with the words, "What's the news, Captain Bates?"

"The seventh day is the Sabbath," Bates replied. Hall accepted the Sabbath, and in the course of time, as an indication of his high regard for the retired sea captain, named his only son Joseph Bates Hall.

Ellen White became acquainted with Joseph Bates probably in the spring of 1846.* He was over thirty-five years her senior. She found him to be, in her words, "a true Christian gentleman, courteous and kind." His Sabbath convictions did not impress her at the outset, as she felt he stressed disproportionately the fourth commandment over the other nine. But about this time she was shown in vision the special sacredness of the fourth commandment in the Decalogue. She and James White, whom she married in August, 1846, studied Bates's Sabbath tract, and before the year was out joined him in observing the seventh-day Sabbath.

At this period the Sabbath question was debated and discussed largely as a legal question only. In time the beauty and spiritual significance of the Sabbath became apparent. To this end Ellen White in her writings contributed not a little. Soon Bates, who had been highly skeptical of Ellen White's visions, witnessed her in one which involved the heavenly bodies. Being competent in astronomy, as a former sea captain, and knowing her lack of formal education, he now accepted the visions of Mrs. White as from God. He said, " 'I believe the work is of God, and is given to comfort and strengthen His "scattered, torn, and peeled people," since the closing up of the work in the world in October, 1844.' "[3]

By 1847 the three pioneer leaders of Seventh-day Adventism, Joseph Bates, James and Ellen White, had found a common ground of faith and belief and were to work closely and effectively together for many years.

In the course of his lifetime Joseph Bates was a sturdy pioneer in many worthy projects. Now he was the first of his erstwhile advent companions to proclaim, in season and out, the Sabbath reform message. In spite of his

---

*Some place their meeting a year earlier, but the evidence seems to favor 1846.

financial plight after having given all of his means to the 1844 movement, his journeys in its behalf took him in the late 1840's throughout New England, New York, and to the Great Lakes region.

Late in 1845 Bates responded to the invitation of Hiram Edson to assist in a conference at Port Gibson, New York. The topics studied at this meeting were the sanctuary and the Sabbath. Bates was particularly interested in the relationship of the two themes. Most of those at this meeting agreed on the Biblical teaching on these subjects; and Hiram Edson, along with others at the meeting, enthusiastically embraced the Sabbath and began to observe it.

From the spring of 1848 until late fall, six conferences dealing particularly with the Sabbath question were held in New England and New York State. Intending to clarify the Sabbath teaching and to bring it and other basic concepts into harmony, the Adventist leaders designed the meetings to reassure the believers and to stimulate the interest and attention of others in this vital subject.

At most of these sessions Joseph Bates lectured on the Sabbath topic and James White on the three angels' messages, including the sanctuary and the spirit of prophecy. About fifty attended the first conference held at Rocky Hill, Connecticut, in April, 1848. Joseph Bates attended virtually all of these conferences. At the Port Gibson conference, with Hiram Edson present, Bates unfolded the Sabbath doctrine. Here, it seems, the Sabbath and the sanctuary teachings became inseparably associated. At some of these meetings the desirability of publishing the views expressed by the group was discussed, but the paucity of funds for the project prevented publishing at this time. Instead, they "resolved, unitedly, to refer it all to God."[4]

On this trip with Ellen and James White, Bates, on getting onto the canal packet on the Erie Canal, missed his footing and fell into the water. This emergency caused the party to stop at the home of friends so that Bates could clean and dry his clothes. They resumed their journey the next day.[5]

The revolutionary upheavals in the year 1848 in various countries of Europe led those still looking for the imminent return of Christ to see in these events further indication of the nearness of the end of all things earthly. Writing at Fairhaven on August 7, 1848, Bates told his good friends Mr. and Mrs. Leonard Hastings of New Ipswich, New Hampshire, "The news from Europe are ominus [*sic*] of the end of all things. It won't do to stop now."

In this same letter Bates tells of his great desire to be out traveling and preaching, but the lack of funds restricted him severely at the time. Some small cash gifts from friends and supporters had been received. His traveling expenses two years before amounted to about twenty-two dollars. He also alluded to calls to "the West" (the Great Lakes region) but felt that financial support would have to reveal the will of God to him in this regard.

In the early summer of 1849 he traveled to the old "Northwest," including Michigan, becoming thus the first to bring the teachings of Sabbath-keeping Adventists to that area. He tried to locate those who had been a part of the 1844 movement and to bring them up to date on the views which he helped shape on the sanctuary question, on the spirit of prophecy in the last days, and above all, on Sabbath reform. From this time on until his death he traveled almost continually near and far, with meager means, enduring hardships in order to preach the message he so fully believed and so deeply loved.

Newly discovered gold in California precipitated a gold fever through the entire United States. But Joseph Bates was intent on winning men and women to what he firmly believed was God's last message for a spiritually destitute world. At this time no Adventists in Michigan—this state of 400,000—worshiped on the seventh-day Sabbath. Bates soon raised up the first group of this kind, at Jackson.

The story of Bates's first convert in Michigan deserves a prominent place in any account of his life. Arthur W. Spalding tells this story in these words: "The first and most prominent of Bates's converts there [in Michigan] was Dan R. Palmer, a blacksmith who with his means was a mainstay of the early work in Michigan, and also the leader in the Jackson church. Bates found him at his forge, and preached his first sermon to the accompaniment of an anvil chorus; for Palmer was not much minded to listen, and would not stop his work. But very soon the message was beating in upon his mind with every hammer stroke. More and more frequent were his pauses while he considered this point and that; and at last, laying down the hammer, and stretching out his grimy hand, he said, 'Brother—what did you say your name was—Bates? You have the truth.' And he invited him to meet the whole company the next Sunday, which he did. But in the meantime Bates visited other members to whom Palmer directed him, and in the end all of them accepted the faith. On Sunday afternoon Palmer took Elder Bates by horse and buggy out into the country to see Cyrenius Smith, a farmer who had not been at the meeting. With equal speed Smith and his family were added to the number of believers; and thus half the foursome, who were later to furnish the backing for establishing the work at Battle Creek, were provided. The other half were Kellogg and Lyon, converts of Cornell and Bates three years later."[6]

5—O.O.A.

A convert to the Sabbath at Jackson wrote to the *Present Truth* to express his thanks to God for "ever inclining Brother Bates's mind to come to Jackson." He said that about forty had accepted the Sabbath. Three years later Bates returned to Michigan to win even greater success in his preaching, and within a decade of his first visit he moved there permanently and devoted the rest of his life to traveling in behalf of the Sabbath message in that region.

Now that he was to recommence a period of intensive preaching, including performing the ordinances of the church such as baptism, one would suppose that somewhere along the way he was set aside or ordained as a gospel minister, but there is no record of ordination. In time he, as a leader in the Seventh-day Adventist Church, was with other leaders issuing credentials to preachers, those who were called to the ministry within the church.

On this point we have this comment from one who has spent years in searching out the facts of early Adventist history: "Many of the workers in the 1844 movement were men ordained in different communions; for in its early proclamation it appealed to hundreds of earnest Christian pastors. Yet there were many laymen who also entered into the preaching without receiving ordination. William Miller himself was licensed, but not ordained, by the Baptists. Some of the Seventh-day Adventists at first were such lay preachers. It does not appear that Joseph Bates was ever ordained or even licensed, though he was active and prominent in the 1844 movement as well as afterward."[7]

During the last half of the 1840's Bates published several tracts in addition to the first one which dealt specifically with the Sabbath. Late in 1846 he wrote a forty-page pamphlet entitled "The Opening Heavens, or a Connected View of the Testimony of the Prophets and Apostles, Concerning the Present and Future Location of the New Jerusalem, the Paradise of God." As the lengthy title indicates, this paper dealt with astronomy, which still held a great appeal for Bates; but its main purpose was to reaffirm the literal coming of Christ at a time when many were rationalizing the disappointment by saying that He had actually come in a spiritual sense. A lady made a striped rag rug and sold it to get funds to aid Bates in publishing this pamphlet. This tract carried an unusual copyright notice which read as follows: "The copyright is secured with Him that sits upon the throne in the coming Heavenly Sanctuary. The grant to use it is unlimited. Those only are punished that abuse the right."

The following year Bates published a pamphlet of eighty pages entitled, "Second Advent Waymarks and High Heaps, or a Connected View of the

Fulfillment of Prophecy by God's Peculiar People, From the Year 1840 to 1847." In this he reviewed the advent movement in the 1840's and stressed the role of providential leadership through all the varied experiences and disappointments of the advent group during these years. A young widow sold her home and gave the money to Joseph Bates to pay the publication costs of this particular pamphlet. His former companion in evangelism, H. S. Gurney, blacksmith from Michigan, made the final payment on Bates's first Sabbath pamphlet. Thus he found support for his various projects from a variety of places, often just in time to enable him to go forward with his plans and travels. Ellen White recorded in her diary the year after Elder Bates's death that "a mother of orphan children of Brother Belden worked with her hands at housework to earn money to give Brother Bates to carry the message to Whitefield, Vermont."[8] Here several accepted the Sabbath teaching from Bates.

Finally in this period Bates published a tract in 1849 under the title, "A Seal of the Living God. A Hundred Forty-four Thousand of the Servants of God Being Sealed in 1849." This was a seventy-two page pamphlet.[9] Here again the sacrifices of a woman made available the finances to enable Joseph Bates to publish an important pamphlet. This tract dealt with the vision of Ellen White at a meeting in Dorchester, Massachusetts, in November, 1849, when Bates was present. This vision clarified the sealing message. The following year Bates printed a sixteen-page pamphlet which took up the typical and antitypical sanctuary.

It is clearly evident that the disappointment in the fall of 1844, overwhelming though it was, did not diminish Joseph Bates's enthusiasm for the religious movement of which he was a vital part. The Sabbath doctrine seemed to energize him anew to preach and teach the people, and in the back of his mind there was the continuing conviction that Christ was at the door and that soon the redeemed would be translated to glory. A letter written by Bates in September, 1849, reflects his undiminished faith in the program. Here is a portion of the letter with the original spelling and punctuation:

"God has manifested His power, . . . heald the sick, cast out devils and caused many to tremble at His mighty power. Ellen had a vision at each conference. The cry from the whole city is Speed the Messengers, Speed the Messengers. The work is not done. Souls are starving. . . . Some souls are dalying and dalying, and trembling to long. . . . The vision says Spare neither money, nor anything, to do the work now. Soon it will be forever to late. . . . I am hastening on with all speed. I held quite an unexpected meeting last evening in Portland, closed and caught my traveling bag and hurried for the boat. I expect to get on shore a few hours of time someplace to hold a meeting with a few hungry ones. The pipes and tobacco are travling out of sight fast, I tell you. Be ye clean that bear the vessels of the Lord. Nothing must be to dear or presious to let go in aid of the Cause now. Oh what a mighty God we have got."[10]

Thus at the midpoint of the nineteenth century Joseph Bates was girding himself anew for the task of bringing to the people of the Northeast, and of the old Northwest region, the message which he cherished above every other possession. Truly he could say of his own efforts, "I am hastening on with all speed."

10

"NEITHER SNOW, NOR RAIN, NOR HEAT, NOR GLOOM OF NIGHT"

(1850-1852)

The mid-century year, 1850, was one of real crisis in the domestic history of the United States. A war had been fought with Mexico, and the vast territories added to the Union in the Southwest raised the ominous question of slavery expansion. There were other issues also, involving the "peculiar institution" in one way or another, such as the returning of fugitive slaves to their owners, and the slave trade in the District of Columbia. These needed to be settled somehow. Some Congressional giants of an earlier day, now nearing life's end, were making a supreme effort to find a compromise that would save the Union. But in fact their era was drawing to a close. The great leaders of the past were one by one reaching the end of their effectiveness as well as of their mortal existence.

Webster, Clay, Calhoun, and others not so well known were seeking to avert the dissolution of the Union which they as national figures had worked so long to preserve, each in his own way. Others stood in the wings ready to move on cue—men like Sumner of Massachusetts, Seward of New York, Douglass of Illinois, and many others. Even the uninfluential occupant of the President's office, General Taylor, was not to survive the critical debates of this summer.

"On 4 July, 1850, . . . President Taylor tried to cool off by consuming an excessive quantity of cucumbers, washed down with copious drafts of iced milk. Washington with its open sewers and flies was always unhealthy in the summer, and the President came down with acute gastro-enteritis, then called *cholera morbus*. He would probably have recovered if left alone, but no President ever had that chance. The physicians in the capital, assisted by a quack from Baltimore, rallied around his bedside, drugged him with ipecac, calomel, opium, and quinine, . . . and bled and blistered him too, until he gave up the ghost on the ninth."[1]

During the course of the summer Congress hammered out a series of agreements and somehow passed them into law, so that the fratricidal conflict was postponed for yet another decade. In the 1850's, new emotional stereotypes were emerging—Uncle Tom, Bully Brooks, Bleeding Kansas, and John Brown, among others—to prepare men's hearts for the dread business of shedding each other's blood. The crisis in the summer of 1850 awakened many people for the first time to the fact that this Union was fragile and that it might be shattered momentarily. The antislavery Quaker poet Whittier wrote:

"Our Union, like a glacier stirred by voices below,
Or bell of kine, or wing of bird, a beggar's crust,
A kindly word may overthrow."[2]

While Joseph Bates had strong antislavery sentiments, he continued with singleness of purpose to proclaim the imminent second coming of Christ and the binding obligation to keep holy the seventh day as the requirement of the law of God, as the sole solution to all men's problems. The measure of his unflagging zeal at this time can be seen in these words which he wrote in 1850: "Reader, . . . in a few days more, our Advocate will have finished his pleading, and God will send forth the seven last plagues, . . . and utterly destroy every soul that is found breaking His commandments."[3]

A striking feature of Bates's activities for the last two decades of his life is his constant itinerating, first in New England and later in Michigan and its neighboring states. A good share of his life he spent on the move, first by sea and later by land, seemingly a compulsive traveler. These itineraries, after 1845 in particular, must impress us, as he had given his modest fortune to the Adventist movement and now was almost totally dependent on the financial largesse of interested friends and those he ministered to.

"The pioneers of the Seventh-day Adventist movement had no fixed abode. They were first of all preachers, evangelists, teachers, and they were itinerant. . . . They went from place to place as the calls came and the Spirit moved. Joseph Bates indeed had a home, that is, a place where his wife stayed; as for him, he ranged back and forth across the land." "Bates was not well fitted to stay at any headquarters. He was the rover, the restless evangelist, who must press on and on, a field officer of the Custer, Jeb Stuart, Patton type, superb in leading, but always at the front."[4]

As previously noted, during Bates's active period as a seaman he spent probably over three fourths of his time away from home. A similar ratio might apply to his travels after 1850. His movements as an itinerant preacher can be followed quite accurately through his letters to the editor published faithfully in the *Review and Herald,* which Bates came to appreciate and support with all his energies. For 1851, for example, one can compile a list of over thirty-five towns, mainly in New England and New York, which he visited. Only rarely does Fairhaven, his hometown, appear as his base in his letters to the *Review and Herald* in this period.

In late August, 1851, he went to Baltimore, Maryland, visiting from house to house for five days. Near the end of October he started out for the West, including Canada West, or Ontario. There he traveled along the Canadian shore of Lake Ontario, and from Toronto north to Simcoe, having previously written from Montreal on New Year's Day, 1852, that he had to walk through deep snow to preach to the "scattered sheep in the back settlements." About February he pushed on to western New York; then he returned to Massachusetts and Fairhaven in March. That summer found him again headed west, this time visiting in Michigan, Ohio, and Indiana. The next year from June until November he visited mainly in the West and started out again one month after his arrival home, itinerating as far as northwest Illinois. On this trip he was absent from Fairhaven for almost six months, traveling as usual "without scrip and without purse."

These journeys characterized his wide range of ministry in the 1850's and 1860's. His frequent time-consuming trips to the Michigan region (train and stage travel from western New York to central Michigan required over thirty-six tedious hours) helped to persuade him to move to Michigan in 1858.

Most of his letters simply report on his travels, with little of a personal nature to add a human touch to the story. Occasionally he casually mentions a point of special interest, such as his contact with the well-known and influential antislavery philanthropist Gerrit Smith of New York. Of this contact he wrote: "In Peterborough, I learned that Gerrit Smith who is so famed for his beneficent acts to the poor, especially to the liberated colored people, was with his companion keeping the seventh-day Sabbath, but not in the message of the third angel, Rev. XIV:12. He listened a little while, said he must

Joseph's personal Bible, kept on display in James White Library at Andrews University, Berrien Springs, Michigan

examine the subject, regretted very much that his companion was absent from home, as she was very much interested in the Advents."[5] Gerrit Smith's biographer confirms the fact that in August 1849 Smith began to observe the seventh-day Sabbath and continued to do so for the remaining twenty-five years of his life.[6]

Bates had been saddened by news of the death of William Miller at Low Hampton just before Christmas, 1849. Two years later he visited the Miller family, on January 1 and 2, 1852, and spoke at the Advent chapel while he was in Low Hampton. His main purpose in the visit, apparently, was to present the seventh-day Sabbath to Miller's widow. Of this effort he wrote, "Sister M[iller] welcomed us, and listened attentively to our explanation of the last message from the chart: said she did not know but the Sabbath which we taught was right."[7] No known evidence indicates that Mrs. Miller ever observed the the seventh-day Sabbath.

In November, 1850, at Paris, Maine, James White published the first issue of what was to survive through the years as the official Seventh-day Adventist church paper, the *Advent Review and Sabbath Herald,* which succeeded the *Present Truth,* of which eleven issues had appeared under White's editorship. At the outset, although Bates approved of publishing as a means of carrying on the work, he apparently felt some misgivings about issuing a regular publication. This, he felt, would unduly tie up the editor and prevent his engaging in other good activities, such as preaching. The other Adventists, "the Laodiceans," he reasoned, were already printing regular periodicals with unsatisfactory results. He preferred to bring out a tract or pamphlet as needed, for ammunition in the battle against their adversaries.

James White wrote at this time that "Brother Bates discouraged me about the paper."[8] Ellen White took note in her diary that "Brother Bates had not the interest in the paper that he should have, and this lack of interest has discouraged James."[9] From the perspective of a decade later, James White could write, "The oldest preacher among us, and almost the only fellow-laborer we then had in this cause, refused for one year to write for our little paper [*Present Truth*], because to publish a paper was to do as others had done who had backslidden."[10] Further consideration by Joseph Bates and counsel from Ellen White led Bates to soften his attitude, however, and beginning with the very first issue of the *Review and Herald,* he wrote for the paper. He continued making regular contributions until his death. On the first issue his name appears with S. W. Rhodes, J. C. Andrews, and James White forming the publishing committee.

From then on he solicited subscriptions to the *Review*. In the first two decades of the publication of the church paper the columns carried over three hundred references to Bates, including articles, but mainly letters by him to the editor, reporting on his preaching missions in which he was undeterred by rain, snow, or subzero temperatures.

Also as early as 1850 Ellen White pointed out several errors being committed by Elder Bates. He did not present in clear light the message of the text "Sell that ye have, and give alms." Also he erred, she pointed out, in praying for the sick in the presence of unbelievers, and in attending the washing of the saints' feet and Communion among unbelievers. He had not made the correct application of Revelation 14:4, and he had destroyed James White's confidence in him. Then she added, "Then I saw Bro. Bates, that he must buckle on the armor."

Also at this time she took Bates to task for failing to go at once to his good friends, the Hastingses, of North Ipswich, New Hampshire, when Mrs. Hastings was critically ill. "If Brother Bates had come directly to your house, she would have been rescued from the grasp of the enemy."

Finally Ellen White concludes, "I saw that the above-named errors of Brother Bates and others more dangerous, brought confusion and had destroyed James's confidence in Brother Bates; I saw that James at first had godly jealousy for the truth, then other jealousy crept in till he was jealous of most every move Brother Bates would make. These wrongs, I saw, must be taken out of the way."

Apparently before long the early leaders were in full harmony again. From Rochester, New York, in June, 1852, Mrs. White could write to the believers at Jackson, Michigan, "Brother Bates is with us. He is coming to see you. . . . His duty is there for the present. I never saw him as free as now. God is with him."[11]

The first issue of the *Review and Herald* contains an article by Joseph Bates on the Laodicean church. In this he refers to his former colaborer, J. V. Himes, and the Albany Conference of 1845, from which Bates deliberately absented himself. His zeal did not permit him to spare even a longtime acquaintance and friend; for of Himes he wrote: "It is vain . . . to attempt to prove that J. V. Himes has not been the leader and leading editor of the *Advent Cause,* for ten years past. This does not prove that he has taken one right step since January 1845. He has led on others to fulfill prophecy, to utter destruction. I pity him, and really wish that his many and deep trials had drawn him to God."[12]

Bates's ministry and message were not universally received with open arms. A candid evaluation by a non-Sabbatarian Adventist presents his labors in a different light. From a letter to the *Advent Herald* by M. L. Clark we read: "We have again been troubled with what we consider to be false teaching, the effects of which are lamentable. About three weeks since, a man by the name of Joseph Bates arrived here by stage, professing to be an Advent preacher, furnished with charts and numerous publications. We had an interview with him, and found his 'message' was the Sabbath, or seventh day, and shut door; that is, except ye keep the seventh day ye cannot be saved. He says the Lord cannot come this year; that the sanctuary in heaven is being cleansed by the blotting out of the sins of Israel; that the seven last plagues are all in the future, which will be the time of trouble, when God will speak, fulfilling Hag. 2:6, 21; that this is a signal for the great battle of God; that the 144,000 sealed (Rev. 14:1) are all the living saints who are sealed by receiving his message, whose sins are blotted out, and who have power over the nations, to execute the judgment written, Ps. 149:9; that then the battle commences, in which the wicked are nearly or quite all slain; that then the Lord comes, and the dead saints are raised, and the living changed; that there is no mercy for sinners, but there is for Advent backsliders. These are the heads of his doctrine as stated by himself, and as we also have found since by his publications."

In reply the editor (Himes) comments, "Captain Bates is an old personal friend of ours, and so far as we know, is better as a man than most of his associates; but we have no confidence in his teaching. He should not be tolerated for a moment."[13]

The hard feelings between the Sabbath-keeping Adventists and those who remained Adventists but rejected the Sabbath flared up again in 1852 also, and later as well. The *Advent Harbinger,* edited by Joseph Marsh, and the *Advent Herald* identified with Joshua V. Himes, levied charges of misrepresentation and false teaching against the Sabbatarians, especially against Joseph Bates. With the passing of time, feelings became more acrimonious between the two groups.

To charges that Bates claimed to be the angel of Revelation 7:2, sealing the servants of God in their foreheads, Bates replied, "Instead of teaching the sealing work before I got the Sabbath, [the facts are] that I kept and taught the Sabbath more than three years before I knew what the sealing work was." He also wrote: "We do not teach that those who keep the first day of the week have the mark of the beast."

That Bates had made some changes in his original position, however, is indicated by his statements on this point. He said: "Since writing the Sealing Message, I have been satisfactorily convinced that the exposition which I then gave of the four messengers standing on the four quarters of the earth, and the ascending, sealing messenger, was incorrect. The difficulties which then prevented me from seeing the clear light on this subject, . . . have since been removed and I now praise the Lord for the clear light that shines; viz., that the four messengers instead of being the four principal governments of earth, are four literal angels commissioned by God to execute His purpose in the destruction of the wicked by His four sore judgments; (or winds;) viz., sword, famine, noisome beasts and pestilence."[14]

In the early years of the mid-century, in spite of frequent travels, Joseph Bates found time, usually during his brief sojourns in Fairhaven, to write articles for the *Review and Herald* other than reports on his travels. These dealt with such topics as the Sabbath, the law of God, prophecy, unlawful marriage, baptism, and the Christian attitude in prayer. His article, "Our Duty to Our Children," must have led him to offer a prayer of thanks for the patience and constancy of his wife Prudence in maintaining a home for the family through the years.

"Time to Commence the Holy Sabbath" found him advocating the observance of Sabbath from six p.m. on Friday to six p.m. on Saturday. This he graciously modified when he heard the sundown-to-sundown concept presented at a later time. The extensive travels of Joseph Bates, his written reports of his work, his Bible study, and his articles such as those cited, give us an insight into the energy and stamina of this pioneer crusader, who slowed up little, if at all, as the advancing years crowded in upon him. In any event, his sixtieth birthday found him not around the family hearth in his snug harbor at Fairhaven, but in western New York with his face pointed even farther west, to attempt even greater exploits for God.

The 1850 Federal census, which for the first time listed names and ages of all living in a given domicile, reveals the following family statistics: Joseph Bates, age 58. Prudence Bates, aged 58 (?). Mary Nye, aged 88 (Prudy's mother). Mary, aged 17. Eliza, aged 29. Joseph Jr. (at sea), aged 20. It also listed in the Bates household William Stott, 60 (mariner); Dianne Stott, 28; Anna Stott, 8. William Stott may have been a seagoing friend of Bates who was down on his luck at the time.

However she managed it, Prudence Bates demonstrated that it takes saintly virtue to live with a saint. Not as quick and decisive in accepting new religious ideas as was her husband, she was not always sure it was faith and not presumption that he displayed when funds were low or nonexistent. When her husband began observing the seventh-day Sabbath in March, 1845, she did not follow him blindly in this, but pondered the matter for five years, until 1850, when she became a Sabbath keeper. Local legend has it that during this period Joseph would drive Prudy to her church on Sunday but refused to attend the services with her on this "unsanctified" day.

The record, including Bates's *Autobiography* and his other writings that are extant, mentions very little about Prudence and the children. The *Review and Herald* in the 1850's carried three letters from her, which give us a glimpse into her own sturdy character and her commitment to God. Writing in December, 1851, she said: "I feel an increasing desire to be filled with all the fullness of God, and the more I strive for this the more I see my own unworthiness. Sometimes I feel almost discouraged, and were it not that the cloud breaks away and a sunbeam of glory illumines my pathway and I claim some precious promise, I should despair. . . . Oh, how I tremble and weep before Him when I think what a poor unworthy creature I am. . . . How precious is Jesus to me, He is my only hope. . . . I love the holy Sabbath better and pray that it may be sanctified to all the dear children who are trying to keep it. I want to be sanctified by obedience to the truth, to be more holy, have a pure heart and clean hands. Pray for me that I may be enabled to overcome by the blood of the Lamb and the word of my testimony."[14]

She again wrote a brief note to the editor of the *Review and Herald* in 1856, deploring her Laodicean condition, but she said she firmly believed that "we have the truth." "He [God] is leading a people, He will guide and guard. . . . Though unworthy, I do hope to be found among that people." And finally, in a longer epistle, the following year, she recalled that for seven years now she had observed the Sabbath. She had failed, she said, to live up to the privileges of children of God. She recalled the "spirit of consecration that was so universal in 1843-44." In closing she appealed for continued faithfulness—"Let us faithfully hold fast our confidence, steadfast even unto the end."[15]

While she wrote the first missive, her husband was battling the cold, the snow, and the "impenetrable hearts" in Canada West. As she wrote the last one, he was still doing battle for the Lord, but this time in the sticky heat of midsummer in Michigan. As the crises in the nation over the extension of slavery into the West developed and deepened, Bates, nothing daunted and with singleness of mind, preached the advent and the Sabbath message.

Mrs. Joseph Bates, née Prudence
Nye, in her later years. Joseph had
known "Prudy" since childhood.

11

THE SEA ROVER PITCHES A TENT

(1853-1855)

The fledgling state of Michigan, which served as a magnet to draw Adventist preachers and leaders at the mid-century, experienced a remarkable growth at this time. From 1840 to 1860 the population more than tripled; it reached three fourths of a million by the time of the Civil War. Most of the citizens descended from the original Canadian immigrants; but many came from Ireland, England, Holland, and Germany—the Irish after the potato famine of 1845, and the Germans after the revolution of 1848. Various religious denominations were represented also, including Mormons who suffered a fate similar to that of Joseph Smith's followers in Illinois at an earlier time.

The population of Michigan concentrated around major centers, which Joseph Bates did not include to any great extent in his itineraries. The people lived largely, though with important exceptions, along the southern portion of the state. Many engaged in agriculture at this time and understandably spread out over a large area. By the time Michigan attained statehood, hunting and trapping were giving way to logging. Soon agriculture would follow, with industry forging ahead in the years after the Civil War.

The common plank roads, while leaving much to be desired, were greatly superior to mudholes and ruts. Three railroads crossed the state, and by 1852 it was possible to go by rail either to Chicago or to New York at what was thought phenomenal speed.

In the summer of 1852 the Michigan Southern and the Michigan Central railroads reached Chicago. Two years later the Great Western completed rail connections from Windsor in Canada (near Detroit, Michigan) to Buffalo, New York. Other railroads were built or extended in the late 1850's as well. All of these internal improvements expedited greatly such itinerant preachers as Joseph Bates and his companions.

Already in the early years of statehood, Michigan showed promise of becoming one of the more populous and progressive states of the Union. This phenomenon coincided with the growing burden of Joseph Bates for the spiritual well-being of the Michigan people.

In the summer of 1852 Bates made his third visit to Michigan, preaching wherever he could gather even a small company and strengthening the groups he had raised up on earlier visits. On this occasion the postmaster in Battle Creek directed him to the "home of the most honest man in town"—David Hewitt. Beginning the day with the Hewitts at breakfast and continuing throughout the day, Bates, with the aid of his ever-present prophetic chart, taught this Presbyterian family his views on the Sabbath and the second advent.

Without vacillation or delay Hewitt and his family accepted the teachings and became the nucleus of Seventh-day Adventist believers in what was to be the official headquarters of the church for many years. Bates, who had been adamant on the question of the "shut door," now realized as did other leaders that the three angels' messages were intended not only for Adventists but also for people of all faiths, or no faith, who in sincerity accepted the teachings. This incident, it appears, marked the end of the "shut door" view among Seventh-day Adventist leaders.

In 1852 Bates also visited Illinois, Wisconsin, and Ohio before returning to Michigan, where he baptized such converts as J. P. Kellogg and M. E. Cornell, who were to prove highly influential in the Seventh-day Adventist Church. In reporting his travels, he mentions finding many troubles in the church in Cleveland at this particular time, difference growing out of various opinions over holding street meetings. He also found much discord in the church in Cincinnati. At Milan, Ohio, an epileptic boy was healed in a highly emotional scene during a three-hour session; and at Perkins, Bates met an old sea captain who had been a fellow prisoner of war with him in Dartmoor.

This man became quite interested in the teachings of Bates. Although at first he refused the books Bates offered him, a little later he did express pleasure in having them. Bates reported that the old captain went out of the place well supplied.

In other areas, such as Sullivan County, Indiana, he found a good interest among the people. Finally after a very heavy season of travel and preaching and much success in making converts, Bates in early October returned to Fairhaven to spend but a single Sabbath with his family before moving off again on a New England itinerary.

Meanwhile the *Review and Herald* continued its mission of supplementing the efforts of the evangelists traveling over the territory. At a conference held at Ballston, New York, at which Joseph Bates was present, in an action taken designed to strengthen and stabilize the publishing work, the conferees voted to purchase a press and other necessary equipment and to publish the *Review and Herald* in Rochester, New York. They named a small committee to receive donations, so that the $600 needed for this action might be realized.[1] By this time a certain affection among the members for the hard-working, sacrificing leaders of the work was developing. Annie Smith, sister of Uriah Smith, wrote a poem characterizing three of the pioneers. This appeared originally in the *Review and Herald,* August 19, 1852, and was subsequently to become a hymn which is even today sung in Seventh-day Adventist churches. A contemporary of Bates reported many years later that this was his favorite hymn.

The first stanza of the three, it was generally believed, describes Joseph Bates in these words:

> "I saw one weary, sad, and torn,
>   With eager steps press on the way,
> Who long the hallowed cross had borne,
>   Still looking for the promised day;
> While many a line of grief and care
>   Upon his brow was furrowed there;
> I asked what buoyed his spirits up,
> 'Oh, this,' said he, 'the blessed hope.'"

Annie Smith's first contact with Joseph Bates in 1851 came about in a remarkable way. Bates was holding meetings in the vicinity of Boston, and one night both Annie Smith and Bates had dreams of seeing each other at this meeting. There was mutual confidence at the outset when these two met, and within three weeks Annie Smith was observing the Sabbath. Her untimely death about five years later deprived the church of a faithful and talented worker. Her brother, Uriah, four years her junior (he had lost his left leg from an illness when he was fourteen), continued on with editorial work

The Sea Rover Pitches a Tent · 81

in the Review and Herald publishing house, writing pamphlets and books until his death half a century later. Here again Joseph Bates influenced young people who in time made contributions to the work of the church.

Two articles by Bates appeared in the *Review and Herald* in the late summer of 1854. These he dispatched from New York State while en route to his labors in Ohio.

In the first article, "Church Order," he traces the characteristics of the true church since apostolic days, stressing the claims of those who preach Christ, His return, and the sanctity of the law, including the Sabbath. This, he insists, constitutes the true church of God in his day. He closes with these words: "My dear brethren and sisters in the Lord, let us all labor for perfect union, harmony and order, in this rising glorious church of God."

His second article, a rather curious one, deals with the prophecy of Nahum 2:3, 4. The "flaming torches" he interprets to be "the lightning trains, speeding their course over the rails at the rate of forty or fifty miles per hour, . . . surely no one will doubt this sign." The shaken fir trees, he reasons, refers to the American buttonwood tree. "Since 1842 I have examined many thousands of the buttonwood tree to satisfy myself with respect to this prophecy." So he concludes the fir trees will be shaken "when the railroad trains will be seen running like the lightnings."

The public mood in New England and throughout the North was greatly excited by the repeal of the historic Missouri Compromise, and of the reports of violence in Kansas over slavery. By degrees the Civil War loomed ever more inevitable. Yet the impending national crisis seems only to have spurred Bates on to proclaim his message. Thus in the summer of 1855 he began to preach in what later were known as "tent efforts."

Bates and an assistant held twelve such meetings in New England during that summer, brief services in each place, with frequent dismantling, moving, and re-pitching of the lecture tent. On the point of longer tent meetings, which were recommended, another student of Bates's life has said: "The biographer, in studying the characteristics of Mr. Bates, would judge that he was not well fitted by nature for tent work as it came into use later. Perhaps the spirit of the sea rover was too strong in his veins. At any rate he seemed ever intent upon traveling here and there, stopping only a day or two at a place. Gradually a feeling arose and was expressed by James White that where the work was intended for non-Adventists, a tent should remain in a town until the new believers were indoctrinated, as the mere inciting of curiosity would avail little."[2]

As a result of this counsel, Bates joined with M. E. Cornell, apparently replacing J. H. Waggoner, in a four-week series of meetings in Hillsdale, Michigan. There had been no Sabbath keepers here, but sixty-six were baptized through the tent meetings of Bates and Cornell.

One acute problem faced by the early Adventist itinerant evangelist was the securing of adequate places in which to hold meetings. The tent relieved the situation somewhat, but it was feasible to use only during the summer season. Even then it was costly to move about and to maintain.

For the most part, preaching services in those days were conducted in the public schoolhouse (with nobody, it seems, raising the church-state issue) or in private dwellings; or, when other churches were favorable, in their meetinghouses. The first house of worship owned by the early Sabbath keepers was one at Buck's Bridge in western New York, which was erected in 1855.

The next meetinghouse was built in Battle Creek, Michigan—a structure measuring 18 x 24 feet and 10 feet high—with upright boards and battens. From about 1855 and onward, Bates increasingly mentions new meetinghouses being built. No doubt this concession to long-range planning and living disappointed Bates and others who were living in constant expectancy of their Lord's imminent return.

One pioneer worker recalled years later a method and procedure for holding meetings in a home, which must have been very familiar to Bates in his various preaching efforts in many places.

"When a 'messenger' came into the neighborhood where a family of Sabbath keepers resided, the largest room in the house was generally fitted up for an evening meeting, by resting the ends of planks on chairs, or blocks of wood, thus providing seating accommodation for all who might come to the meeting. Every other business was then laid aside, and a personal invitation was extended to everyone for miles around to come and hear about the Lord's coming.

"Few fine-spun theories were then brought forward; for they were unknown. But in the most simple manner attention was called directly to the prophecies, tracing events from ancient times to the present. By the aid of a chart illustrating the prophetic symbols, which every preacher carried with him in those days, these things never failed to create a deep interest."[3]

The building of the many plain and small meetinghouses by the Seventh-day Adventist believers was only one of the indications pointing to the need for a more comprehensive organization of the church. The necessity of having an official body to hold legal title to such properties became apparent to men like James White, although the idea was opposed by many others. Bates usually played the role of moderator in the various meetings held, which culminated in the formal organization of the Seventh-day Adventist Church in 1863.

12

YEARS OF TRANSITION

(1856-1858)

The last half of the 1850's was a time of transition for Joseph Bates and for the entire advent movement. Leaders undertook steps to organize the work and workers without creating another "Babylon" or "ecclesiastical despotism." A beginning had been made before 1855 by issuing cards to those engaged in public ministry, a forerunner of ministerial papers or credentials, cards signed by James White and Joseph Bates as leading ministers. At successive conferences the matter of a legal organization for operating the publishing work and for holding church property was studied and plans were adopted. A program of helping evangelists financially, at least in a token way, was adopted following discussions of systematic benevolence, and specifically the tithing principle. In all these developments Joseph Bates was intimately involved, usually serving as chairman of these conferences.

Although his face and feet seemed to turn more and more toward the west, specifically to Michigan, Bates spent most of the year 1855 traveling and preaching in New England and New York. Beginning in Fairhaven and nearby Dartmouth, he labored in south and central Massachusetts, in Connecticut, and then in northern New England and New York. Back in Fairhaven in early summer, he appealed for literature to place aboard whaling ships bound for the South Pacific.[1]

By late fall he was back in Michigan, where he escaped serious injury or death when his train was derailed (a frequent event in those early days of the railroads) en route to Chicago. Bates remained in the Michigan area all winter and spring, concluding his visit by presiding as chairman of a conference in Battle Creek which voted to request that Elders Smith, White, and Waggoner prepare a Sabbath School tract in German. Early June 1856 found him back home at Fairhaven after being absent since the previous autumn. He thanked God for caring for his family and reported that the churches at Fairhaven and Dartmouth were doing well.

A reading of Bates's letters published in the *Review* during this period reveals his unflagging devotion. As he was leaving Battle Creek late in October, 1856, a storm left him stranded with a family with which he was not acquainted. However, he lost no time in studying the Bible with them, and his visit stirred their interest in his teachings. While itinerating in Iowa that same year, he visited J. N. Andrews at Waukon, Iowa, where Andrews was recuperating from an illness. In spite of his continual traveling he found time to write, and in the fall of 1856 the *Review* carried his four-part series, "The Kingdom of God."[2]

A communication in the *Review* from Mrs. Bates about this time expressed thanks to the sisters at Battle Creek for the eight dollars sent to the Bates family. She wrote, "The brethren have my thanks for the interest they have taken for my dear husband, that they have helped him 'after a godly sort.'" This letter is followed by a note from Ellen G. White in which she commends the sacrifice of the workers: "Sisters, we can do something in this matter. We can deny ourselves of articles we do not actually need—wrought collars, undersleeves, 'stomachers,' Ec., which are expressly forbidden in God's Word. Isa. iv." The last paragraph of this article by Mrs. White reads, "Our dear Bro. and Sr. Bates deserve our prayers, sympathy and support. We will remember them in their self-denial and sacrifice, and see that their wants are well supplied."[3]

From time to time in letters to the paper, words of appreciation for the ministry of Joseph Bates appear. Illustrative of these is one from Jessie Dorcas of Freemont, Ohio. "I would say to your esteemed Brother Bates [through the *Review*] that I received your kind letter and know not how to be grateful enough for his kind care for me."

The Monterey church began increasingly to attract Bates's attention. During the severe winter of 1856-1857, before he turned to labor in eastern Michigan, his letters to the editor of the church paper indicate that he spent time in and around Monterey each month from November 1856 to February 1857. In spite of extremely cold weather, people traveled six to ten miles, going and coming, to attend the meetings. One account is of particular interest and reveals the depth of dedication of those who accepted the teachings of Joseph Bates. "On First-day morning, [mercury 30 degrees below zero] some of the Brn. in the time of service cut and sawed out the ice some three feet thick, and found water of sufficient depth, wherein seven souls were buried with Christ in baptism. The church attended to the ordinances of the Lord's house, and were much strengthened and blessed of the Lord."[4] Bates, who apparently officiated at this service, was sixty-five years of age.

Indicative of the consistent, if only moderate, success he was having in winning people to the advent faith is a typical letter in the *Review* from Mary Armstrong of Waverly, Michigan. She expresses her appreciation for the ministry of Elder Bates on two Sabbaths, and mentions that seven were baptized and as many more came out for the Sabbath during this period.

Arriving in Battle Creek in the spring of 1857, Bates served as chairman of a conference which dealt with several urgent matters, among them the purchase of a power press for the *Review*. The conference approved a resolution to build an adequate meetinghouse in Battle Creek, and support was voted for the tent work at this meeting, which was harmonious throughout. Cautions were sounded against creating prejudice by conduct or argument.

That summer Elders Bates and J. H. Waggoner held tent meetings in Michigan. These were of two or three weeks' duration, using the Michigan tent. Later, in Vermont, they held meetings in a borrowed tent. They held these meetings consecutively at Burlington Village, where thirteen were baptized in spite of stormy weather; Union City, with some assistance from James and Ellen White; and at Burr Oak, with inclement weather and spiritualists attempting to frustrate their best efforts.

Other leaders had counseled holding longer series of meetings than those of just a few days or nights, as Bates had been doing. The use of a tent as a meeting place provided mobility and apparently novelty. Except for the problems of stormy weather, the large tent was used to good effect in many places over a period of many years by Adventist evangelists.

Following is a description of the way this type of evangelism operated: "The tent was of a circular form about sixty feet in diameter. When it had been brought to the place arranged for, which might very likely be a pasture adjoining a public road, the first thing to do was to select a suitable tree for the center pole. Often this would be a pine or an oak. After it had been cut down and trimmed, the neighbors' help would be obtained in bringing it to the perpendicular position, after which the canvas was duly raised, the side poles put in place, and the platform, pulpit, and seats added. The seats consisted of boards laid across other boards set edgewise, and fastened by stakes. To begin with, there were no backs; but later it was customary, at least in the case of seats near the front, to furnish backs formed by boards nailed to upright stakes. The platform was about two feet high, and built up at the front about four feet high and eight or ten feet long, to serve as a desk. This was often covered with cloth. Behind this the speaker stood. Along the entire front of the platform ran a table consisting usually of one long wide board, properly supported, on which was displayed a variety of books, tracts, and pamphlets. These were always well advertised at the close of the meeting, and as soon as the benediction had been pronounced, the people would come forward, curious to examine the publications.

"In some of the more important efforts, it was quite customary for the work to be carried on by two preachers, speaking on alternate nights; but laborers were scarce, and a great many excellent tent-meetings were carried on by only one preacher with the aid of a tent-master."[5]

From an undated letter near the end of October, 1857, we learn that Bates finally arrived back home at Fairhaven, presumably earlier that month, as he was still in Michigan in mid-September. In one of his infrequent references to his family he mentions, without furnishing details, that his daughter's health was improving slowly. This daughter was presumably Mary, although Eliza was not married until the following year and may have still been living at home. He also states that his only surviving son, now a young man of twenty-seven and still a whaler, had recovered from injuries suffered when thrown from his boat by a whale.[6]

From the excellent collection of handwritten abstracts of whaling voyages in the Melville Whaling Room of the New Bedford Free Public Library, we learn the additional facts that the younger Bates was first mate on the *Golconda,* of New Bedford, and that the accident occurred out of the port of Patia, Peru, in July, 1857.

With characteristic urgency for the task and a special burden for the work in Michigan particularly, Joseph Bates set out again for a six-month tour which took him to Michigan, Indiana, New York, and northern New England before the familiar faces and sights of Fairhaven came again into his view.

Somehow, in the midst of his many other activities, Bates found time to write a sketch of his early life for publication in the *Youth's Instructor,* beginning in November, 1858. In this he was encouraged by his friends in and around Michigan. The series, eventually consisting of fifty-one articles, ran for five years in the youth paper. Later it appeared in book form, titled *Autobiography*,* and was issued again after his death under the editorship of James White.

Bates filled his customary role as chairman of a conference in Battle Creek on November 6, 1857. The records of this meeting reveal that the cost of the new meetinghouse for Battle Creek was $881.39 and that less than a third of the amount still had to be raised. The conference named a committee of seven men to attend to the financial needs of ministers, so that they could devote all their time to the ministry, and authorized the amount of $2,000 to be raised for this committee to administer for this purpose. The conference also appointed a revision committee to see that all published material properly represented the church.[7] Thus it appears that the church was progressing toward organization, the earlier fears giving way to the realization that such a move was necessary.

What thoughts passed through Joseph Bates's mind as he presided at these meetings we can only conjecture. It is certain his one consuming passion now, as it ever had been since he accepted the advent message in the early days, was the speedy return of Christ to this earth. But the Christlike and cooperative spirit of Joseph Bates led him to work with his brethren in developing these early organizational features of what was in just a few years to become the Seventh-day Adventist Church.

---

*This book has recently been reprinted by the Southern Publishing Association.

13

WESTWARD THE COURSE OF ADVENTISM

(1858-1860)

The travels of Joseph Bates in the decade before the American Civil War indicate that the advent message was moving westward with the rest of the nation. Bates was spending more and more of his time in and near Michigan. So were his ministerial colleagues, White, Andrews, Loughborough, Byington, Smith, and others.

One might speculate on the reasons for this. Were the people there more responsive to the preaching of Bates and his co-workers? What was the attraction in that direction? The other two of the early Adventist triumvirate, Ellen and James White, also supported this trend. James White advised the believers to go west and add strength to the movement there. Ellen White wrote:

"I saw that God has been opening the way for the spread of present truth in the West. It requires much more power to move the people in the East than in the West, and at present but very little can be accomplished in the East. Special efforts should be made at the present time where most good will result.

"The people in the East have heard the proclamation of the second coming of Christ, and have seen much of the display of the power of God, and have fallen back into a state of indifference and security where it is almost impossible to reach them at present. . . .

"I saw that the people in the West could be moved much more easily than those in the East. They have not had the light of the truth, and have not rejected it, and their hearts are more tender and susceptible to the truth and the Spirit of God."

"I saw that special efforts should be made in the West with tents; for the angels of God are preparing minds there to receive the truth. This is why God has moved on some in the East to move to the West. Their gifts can accomplish more in the West than in the East. The burden of the work is in the West, and it is of the greatest importance that the servants of God should move in His opening providence."[1]

For these and other reasons Joseph Bates decided to live in Michigan, making the move in 1858, although the record of his ministerial labors hardly shows a break to allow for the necessary duties in carrying out such a major move. Probably his wife, Prudence, bore the brunt of the burdens of moving in May of 1858.

The apparent ease with which Bates pulled up his roots in New England, roots extending back for his whole lifetime and beyond to those of his forebears, provides evidence of his complete disdain for the things of this life which figure so prominently in the plans and actions of most people. The record gives no hint that Bates ever returned, even for a visit, to New England, although Prudence went back to visit friends and family in the New Bedford area during the summer of 1863. In a letter to his sister Harriot in 1868 Bates expressed the hope of visiting New England again.

Rather than settle in Battle Creek, as did most of the workers who moved to Michigan, Bates chose the outskirts of the rural community of Monterey, northwest of Battle Creek. Here he made his home in a modest house for the fourteen years until his death. When he was at home, he actively participated in his local church, which was within walking distance from his home. Both he and Mrs. Bates are interred just a short distance from their home in the countryside near Monterey.

At this point, before following Bates's activities during this time, it might be of interest to trace a brief history of the work in Monterey.

As early as 1853 M. E. Cornell had preached in the schoolhouse at Monterey and had help to raise up a group. Within three years the group had organized a church of more than forty members and erected a meetinghouse. The following year James and Ellen White visited the Monterey community, and in a schoolhouse where a service was held during her visit Ellen White had a vision which made the occasion memorable for all in attendance. The work at Monterey seems to have been of special interest and concern to James and Ellen White as well as to Joseph Bates.

The Joseph Bates family home in Monterey, Michigan, from 1858 to 1872.

The spiritual condition of the church members there, as elsewhere, fluctuated from time to time. A year after moving there, Bates reported that the members "were pressing forward for victory and eternal life." More often than not the church prospered. The members, according to a former pastor in the area, Bert Van Horn, were a prosperous group. "The brethren in Monterey were well-to-do, and liberal in their offerings to the cause."[2] However, in a vision in 1860 Mrs. White said, "The brethren [in the Monterey church] are between truth and the love of the world." She then singled out certain members, calling them to a higher individual standard of Christian living and conduct.[3]

In 1862 a new church edifice was erected at Monterey, and the membership remained just under a hundred. At one time reports arrived that the religious ideas of the Monterey members led to insanity in some of their members. Even the Detroit newspapers carried such reports, but they were vigorously denied. The *Review* put out a leaflet on the subject, but no copies appear to be extant today. An unnamed member of the Monterey church reported on its state in 1866:

"During the past year the church has dismissed fourteen members. Some of them have moved to other churches, and two have died. Nine have been added. The church now has seventy-eight members in its communion, all of whom, with very few exceptions, meet at our established place of worship every Sabbath. We also hold two stated evening prayer and conference meetings every week, and a female prayer meeting on First-day afternoon. In connection with our Sabbath services, we have organized Bible classes and a very interesting Sabbath School of fifty-six scholars, and have a library of selected books for both parents and children. With these needed forms of godliness we desire power to enable us to overcome the world, the flesh, and the devil. With regard to dress and how to live, and laying aside every wrong and filthy habit, we are resolved to go forward."[4]

An interesting document dealing with the Monterey church in the 1860's is in the library of Andrews University in Michigan. The influence of Joseph Bates, for so long identified with this church and active in its program, can be seen in this document, "Records of the Seventh-day Adventist Church, Monterey, Michigan." Covering events beginning in 1860 and concluding in 1872, the year of Joseph Bates's death, it speaks eloquently through the statistics of this church. In the annual report for February 10, 1871:

Additions (to membership)—none
Losses—dead, one
Losses—apostasy, seventeen
Number at beginning of year—ninety-six
Number at close of year—seventy-eight
S. S. scholars—forty

These records indicate that the church dealt sternly with those known not to be living in full harmony with its teachings. In presiding at some of the meetings when strict discipline was administered, Joseph Bates undoubtedly approved of and probably helped to mold what seems today to be harsh treatment of erring members. His concept of the high privilege of church membership caused him and the body of members to feel that they would be delinquent in their responsibility if they did not deal drastically with offenders against the law of God and the principles of the church.

Typical of church actions are those recorded of a meeting held on August 2, 1863:

"No. 3. It was voted that we withdraw the hand of fellowship from Eleanor Wilcox for violating the Sabbath.

"No. 4. Noted that we withdraw the hand of fellowship from M. Goodall, for violating the Sabbath.

"No. 5. Voted that we withdraw the hand of fellowship from Amanda Wilcox for walking disorderly.

"No. 6. Voted that we withdraw the hand of fellowship from Lydia Durand for violating the Sabbath, walking disorderly, and acting as a busybody."

The record book of this early church from time to time also reports the review of all members and specific votes of continuing fellowship in the church. It even reviews Joseph and Prudence Bates's progress in the Christian way. The following record under date of May 17, 1870, about three months before Mrs. Bates's death, quotes Joseph Bates as stating before the committee: "I am in harmony with this work and enjoying some of the blessing of the Lord. I feel the Lord has helped in these meetings. I believe in all points of the truth, have been in this work since 1839, am established in the Testimonies, have been acquainted with them for twenty-five years, am living the reforms as well as I can, am in harmony with all the church." Brother Bates was unanimously received.

The next entry quotes Sister P. M. Bates. "Have been in the message since 1850, am in harmony with all points of the truth. I believe the Testimonies and am trying to live accordingly, am in harmony with all members of the church." Sister Bates was unanimously received.

W. H. Littlejohn, presumably the pastor at this time, took charge of this review of the members' spiritual standing. He conducted a revival series at Monterey in May, 1870, and conducted Joseph Bates's funeral two years later. That Bates endorsed the membership canvass is apparent from this report in the church paper. "We feel deeply indebted to him [Elder Littlejohn] for his faithful, impartial, and judicious management of the cases of every member as their names were called from the church record. It was manifest that the Lord blessed and strengthened him for this work."[5]

Finally these handwritten minutes of this church, so intimately tied in with Joseph and Prudence Bates, offer additional testimony of the fact that they were largely dependent upon the church members and friends to supply their needs. In this record book, actions appear from time to time authorizing firewood and a shelter for the wood at the Bates home. On August 5, 1860, entry records the vote "that the church pay what is due on Brother Bates's house out of the SB [Systematic Benevolence] fund."

The decennial census of 1860 records the value of the Bates home at $400. A handwritten undated letter (written presumably about 1857, shortly before he moved to Michigan) entitled "To the Church in Monterey and Allegan" and signed by Joseph Bates, says in part, "I am very much obliged to you for the twelve dollars you sent . . . to buy me a coat. I needed one about this time about as much as any garment I ware [sic] as I have been laboring mostly in new places for some time where the wants of messengers are not much thought of. They may be one reason why you have been led to inquire into my wants."[6] Ellen White wrote in her diary on February 4, 1859, as follows: "Went to the stores with Brother Bates and Augusta Bognes. They purchased a coat for Brother Bates."[7] This was presumably a later but similar transaction.

In the same month during which he made the move to Michigan, Bates presided as chairman (because of the indisposition of James White) at a Battle Creek conference which authorized the purchase for $400 of another sixty-foot tent. The record contains a warning against the activities of one G. Cranmer and refers other items to a committee of one, namely James White. Bates spent the rest of the year in Michigan and adjoining states, reporting problems and reverses, but mainly progress and success. Particularly successful was the work at Lapeer, Michigan, where within four months of the first tent meeting held there a new church was dedicated with thirty-one members and a growing interest.

During 1859, when suspicions and estrangement between North and South were increasing, Joseph Bates maintained as strenuous a traveling schedule as ever, preaching and baptizing new members as he went. This year he worked mainly in Michigan, but was still rarely at home. Although he was beyond what today is normally considered retirement age, nothing seemed to have stopped the indomitable crusader or deterred him from his "appointed rounds." In his reports he did not disguise the fact that there were problems and obstacles to face along the way, and that in places there was much opposition, often from ministers of other churches.

In his report dated May 9, 1859, from Tompkins, he mentions an uproar at Onondaga a few days before. But in Tompkins the story was different. Ten were baptized there. He alludes to one of these in a rather queerly constructed and involved passage: "After the rainstorm abated we repaired to the waterside, where ten, who had become dead to the law, were married to Christ by being buried with Him by baptism into death, that they should walk in newness of life. One of the number is girding up his loins and lighting his lamp, and shaping his course to reach a station with the watchman on the walls of Zion to join them in sounding the alarm in God's holy mountain, to all inhabitants of the land, and close up the final warning with the loud cry of the Third Angel's Message."[8]

In early June he chaired a conference in Battle Creek which adopted the plan of systematic benevolence presented by James White. Referring to this meeting Joseph Bates wrote: "Thank God for the interesting and important conference of Sabbath keepers that has just closed. It was decidedly the best one I ever attended. It was a refreshing from the holy of holies. God's people have turned their faces homeward again, rejoicing in the God and Rock of their salvation. The messengers of God are pressing their way again into the wide harvest field, to draw out the residue of the little flock; viz., the hundred and forty-four thousand to stand on Mount Zion with their redeeming Lord. All hands are at their stations in the office, getting forward the *Review, Instructor,* and the little winged messengers [books] through the power press, scattering light and truth from God's great book of directions to all the scattered remnant of God. The King's business is urgent and pressing. Tarry not in all the plains! 'Remember Lot's wife.' Your brother in the blessed hope, J. B."[9]

Again in August in Battle Creek, Bates presided over a business meeting of the Battle Creek Church, which approved assistance for widows and orphans and encouraged members to support the missionary fund and the workers in the field. Financial support was also voted to assist Elders Hull and Cornell in Iowa, to provide them with literature for their work. Early autumn found Bates, accompanied by a small band of converts, traveling six miles out of Green Bank in wind and heavy rain in search of a stream suitable to baptize seven believers.

Soon after this Bates suffered what seemingly was his first serious and prolonged illness. At Conway, Michigan, he suffered with "fever and ague" to such an extent that he was unable to preach—a rare and painful experience for this dauntless evangelist. When he arrived in Jackson after a three-hour ride on a freight train, he took the water pail in the station and "drank water enough to quench, in part, the fire that seemed to be consuming my very vitals."[10] At Jackson he met his wife and remained there for over three weeks, till November 11. There he regained his strength, and on the twelfth he was at work, going first to Tompkins and then to Parma.

For the next six weeks and more, until early January, Bates's communications in the *Review* do not appear. This may indicate a period of recuperation at his home at Monterey, or perhaps a period of less strenuous activities.

14

A CHURCH IS BORN

(1860-1863)

In the fateful year of 1860 when the nation, now emotionally aroused for war, teetered on the brink of a bloody fratricidal conflict, Joseph Bates kept on traveling and preaching, even when storms in February and March made the roads well-nigh impassable.

In early summer he chaired a conference at Caledonia, Michigan. Here the delegates resolved that all Michigan churches should support the tent operations during the summer season and that the Widow Cranston was worthy of sympathy and support by the churches and brethren. The cash raised for each of these projects may indicate the value placed on evangelism as compared with welfare—sixty-three dollars for the tent, and ten dollars and sixty-six cents for the Widow Cranston.

In his itinerant preaching Bates was confronted in one place with the prejudice of a Mr. Cranmer, who was preaching the second coming and the seventh-day Sabbath, but not the visions of Mrs. White or the sanctuary, as Bates was doing. This was apparently Gilbert Cranmer, who was refused a license to preach because he would not quit using tobacco and also because of certain home problems as well. He went out on his own and preached. His few followers among Seventh-day Adventists formed a group which permitted the use of tobacco and countenanced certain other practices disapproved by the main body of believers.[1]

In another area, O. R. L. Crozier, who had been trailing Bates in his journeys, was teaching that the law was done away with. Crozier had earlier

A Church Is Born · 97

argued convincingly for the Sabbath. Finally in late summer Bates was confined again with "fever and ague," a condition which lingered for several weeks. We find little record of his activities from late June until the end of September. On August 29 he wrote that he had to decline an invitation from William Appleton in Greenville to assist in defending the faith against Methodists, Baptists, and Congregationalists. Declining an invitation of this type would indicate that his health problem was real indeed, as had he been in reasonably good health he would have hastened to the fray.

Bates chaired a highly significant conference at Battle Creek beginning on the evening of September 29, 1860. Uriah Smith served as secretary. Fortunately, a rather lengthy report of this important meeting, apparently taken down stenographically, was published in the *Review*.[2] A spirited discussion on church organization emerged. George I. Butler, who later served at two different times as president of the General Conference, opposed, he said, anything that was not in the Bible. Others opposed any legal organization, supporting only a loose, New Testament type of church.

After extended consideration of the subject, the name Seventh-day Adventist was finally approved as a recommendation to the churches. Elder Butler dissented, and four others including J. N. Andrews did not vote. Thus almost three years before the church as such was organized as a legal entity, it had a name that described its two most distinctive teachings.

On November 14, 1860, Bates returned home to Monterey after an absence of seven weeks. While he was on this journey among the churches at Owosso, Lapeer, Ionia, and other towns, the nation had gone to the polls to elect a President. Four main candidates confronted the voters, among them Abraham Lincoln. His election determined the course of history during the next few years and for future generations. But on election day, November 6, Joseph Bates was in Ionia preaching the Word to the people who, he felt, needed salvation more than they needed any political panacea or deliverer.

The official decennial census of that year, 1860, lists Joseph Bates as an Adventist minister, and his wife Prudence. No children or other dependents were named as residing with them on this date. His only remaining unmarried daughter, Eliza, had been married in 1858 to Captain George H. Taber,* who traced his ancestors—Francis Cooke, Richard Warren, and others—to

---

*He lived into the twentieth century. Descendants of Eliza Bates and George Taber are living in New York, Pennsylvania, and Oklahoma. Mrs. Bates's mother, Mary Nye, died April 6, 1852, in Fairhaven at the age of eighty-six.

the Mayflower. The census records the value of Bates's real estate at $200 and his personal estate at $100. As we remember the extent of his financial holdings upon his retirement from the sea, these figures tell us something significant about this great and good man and about his equally great and good companion of forty-two years. Virtually all they had went to support the Adventist cause. In the light of this census report which lists no dependents in his family, or others living in his domicile, it is difficult to know his meaning when he writes at this time that he received word while in Caledonia that his family were all sick at his home, since his only surviving son was a whaler, presumably at sea, and his three daughters had been married and had their own homes in other parts of the country.

Joseph Bates was particularly successful in studying the Bible with small groups and pressing for a decision from his hearers. One who met him late in Bates's life wrote thus on this point:

"His method of teaching the message was peculiar to him. He did not wait for an audience in some public building, though he had the power to interest large gatherings. But upon finding a friendly home in some community, as soon as he settled, he would invite the family to a study from the Bible. Then hanging up his prophetic chart, he would cover the world's history in prophetic outline so tersely and earnestly as to convince his hearers of the truth in a single study. He knew nothing about many side issues by which to draw the mind toward the truth, yet his work was often far-reaching in effect."[3]

Another respected denominational leader and chronicler of the early church compares Bates with James White, his companion in service: "Joseph Bates . . . was equally a pioneer with him, equally a discoverer of foundation truths, equally assiduous in evangelism, and more than his equal in the opening of new fields and in advancing the message.

"Nor was Bates lacking in executive ability. In those days, when the whole Adventist world was hypersensitive to the suggestion of organization, when they were, in Bates's frequent phrase, as 'sheep upon the mountains,' he was diligent in searching them out and binding them together in 'bands.' His influence with them was supreme; the disciples wept when he left them. And when the brethren came together in conferences, if Father Bates was there, he was sure to be their presiding officer. Indeed, when at last, in 1860, the brethren came to a mind to organize, Joseph Bates it was who sat in the chair and guided the conference. But, on the whole, Bates was not well fitted to stay at any headquarters."[4]

During the winter of 1860-1861, while seven Southern states were seceding from the Union, Bates held meetings at Monterey with James and Ellen White in attendance. He reported that there existed a good spirit in the church at this time, with three fourths of the congregation making a solemn covenant to obey God. Following this period at his home church, Bates held meetings for three weeks at Orange, Ionia County, Michigan. Despite bad weather, converts were made and seven were baptized in a stream where a hole had been cut in the ice. Before he left Orange, fifteen had joined the church. Word came that his family was ill; so he returned home, to find that they were improving. Setting out again, this time for Ionia, he missed the train at Ada. As one would expect, he set about to hold meetings in Ada. When later he was detained at Wayland by impassible roads, he, nothing daunted, preached to the people at Wayland.

Toward the end of April a small conference was held at Battle Creek, with Bates, as usual, chosen chairman. The first item of business dealt with the organization of the publishing association to conform with recent state legislation on the subject. In harmony with the action naming the church organization the year before, the conference voted to designate the press as the Seventh-day Adventist Publishing Association. Before the close of the second session, this conference in a lengthy action unanimously voted to exhort preachers and laity to put away from their speech all that which was trifling and tended to excite mirthfulness. The need for this action may have indicated a condition of less urgency and less sobriety than in the earlier days of the movement. Also coming on the heels of the attack on Fort Sumter and the official beginning of hostilities between North and South, it may have reflected the serious crisis in the nation. Whatever inspired the action, it reads as follows:

"*Whereas,* In our opinion, remarks calculated to excite mirthfulness tend to grieve the Holy Spirit from our midst and thus deprive us of the guidance of heaven in our deliberations, therefore

"*Resolved,* That we consider it a breach of order to indulge in such remarks. We request the chairman to call to order any who may use them.

"*And whereas,* In view of the solemn time in which we are living, the *holy,* solemn message we profess, the importance of using 'sound speech,' and 'words that shall administer *grace* to the hearers,' and in view of the fact that God's word condemns in the most unequivocal terms the use of trifling thoughts and words, even declaring that 'for *every idle* word that men shall speak they shall give account thereof in the day of judgment,' therefore

"*Resolved* (1.) That this conference assembled, both preachers and lay members, covenant together to put away from us, whether in preaching or in social relations, all lightness and trifling. (2.) That we recommend to our brethren scattered abroad, to pursue a similar course and rid themselves of this blighting sin which drives the Spirit of God from the heart of His people."[5]

Finally, among the specific local actions, the conference voted to request ministers assembled at the conference to write an address on the subject of church organization. Thus it appears that more and more attention was being directed to this theme, in light of the growing membership, the activities of unauthorized preachers in the field, and the necessity of a more permanent organization.

The gravity of the nation's plight must have weighed heavily on the minds of Bates and his colleagues, especially after the disaster at Bull Run on July 21. A few days later Bates noted that he spent a day of humiliation, fasting, and prayer in Monterey, presumably in light of the North's reverses.

In March of 1861 a testimonial by Bates in support of James and Ellen White appeared in the *Review*. He referred to the severe setbacks and trials they had experienced and asked the support of all the members for them.

Early in October, 1861, Bates in Battle Creek chaired another conference for Michigan, where good progress was being made on a new publishing house. The conference discussed the problem of organizing the church without a creed. They agreed finally on a simple signed covenant without a creed. At this meeting the Michigan Conference was organized. Officers were named, including Joseph Bates as chairman. Seven other local conferences were formed in 1862 along similar lines.

Before this year was out, Bates's home church at Monterey formally organized with fifty members. Since the group was first started in 1855, twenty had been disfellowshiped. For four months from the time of organizing the Monterey church, until March 10, the letters of Bates reporting on his itineraries did not appear, whether because of illness in the family or other reasons, but in late April we find him driving seven miles to find a place near Wright, Michigan, to baptize new converts, an incident he regarded as an ordinary duty. That summer, at the age of seventy, Bates assisted his home church in Monterey in framing and erecting a new meetinghouse.[6] A letter in the *Review* reminds us of Bates's trip many years earlier to Canada. From Whitby, J. Hebner expresses thanks for Bates's visit there years before, at which time he joined the movement. Bates was still engaged in a similar work and reported that at Saint Charles and also at Pine Creek many were weeping and sobbing in the meeting. At Saint Charles the people sang at the baptism, "Thou hast said, exalted Jesus, take thy cross and follow Me."

Bates presided at the first annual session of the Michigan Conference with credentialed delegates from the churches, held in the new Monterey church, October 4-6, 1862. Attended by almost five hundred believers from Michigan, New York, Ohio, Indiana, and Wisconsin, this was the largest group of Seventh-day Adventists ever assembled up to that time. White, Loughborough, and Hull were the principal speakers.

At this session "the churches of Michigan were accepted into the Conference, officers were elected, and credentials were voted to workers. Questions brought for consideration to the Conference related to (1) divorce; (2) the ordination of preachers from other faiths; (3) young preachers baptizing before ordination. The divorce question was referred to the Conference Committee. Ministers joining from other faiths must be re-ordained. No minister could baptize before his ordination."[7]

Seventeen churches sent official representatives to this meeting, and these were united by actions taken. The conference voted to meet a year later at Battle Creek, extending an invitation to the newly organized state conferences to attend. Before that time, however, leaders felt that the meeting should be held the next spring rather than waiting until fall. At this meeting the credentials of Bates and the conference ministers were renewed.

Bates seems to have used and relished certain expressions, some of which have come down to us to the present time. Others are rather representative of the man. Some of his interesting expressions are "We had a sweet, melting time," "higher and holier ground," "to meet the coming storm," and "before the dreadful storm that is now gathering."

For the first half of 1863 the reports of Bates do not appear. In September he met his wife in Detroit. She was just returning from a summer in New England, visiting her family and friends. The reference to her improved health suggests that Bates may have restricted his travels early in 1863 in order to care for her. Beginning at Jackson on July 6, he was unusually active again, even working in Northern Indiana, where he was joined by the Byingtons at Churchill. He reported that there were some indulging in "the use of tobacco and hoops who resolved that they could break away from their idols."

In May 1863 occurred a decisive event in the history of the Seventh-day Adventist Church. Bates was on the scene. A General Conference session was called, and met at Battle Creek May 20-23 of that year. It was the first such meeting, with representatives present from six state conferences—all the new conferences except Vermont. The conference adopted a constitution and elected officers. John Byington, whom Joseph Bates had influenced to join the Adventist Sabbatarians, was called to serve as the first president of the General Conference, after James White had declined.

The year after Byington was elected president of the General Conference, Ellen White took him to task for his attitude toward Bates on an earlier occasion. She wrote, "Since that house was purchased for Brother Bates to live in, you have been sinking. . . . You ought to have been foremost in the matter, and cheerfully, gladly helped in getting a home for him instead of having the least trial in the matter." However, she was impartial in her reproof and the same year in a letter to "Dear Brother Ingraham" she charges him and the Bates family with being suspicious regarding James White's "manner of dealing." Also he had "spread prejudice all around against us, and did not keep it from unbelievers."[8]

There was a sharp division among the leaders as to the wisdom of setting up a church organization. The subsequent growth and prosperity of the church has demonstrated the wisdom of the move. Through all the give and take of debate on the issue, "Bates was well known as an organizer."[9] In fact, as early as 1853 deacons were elected in his home church at Fairhaven, proving that he was sensitive to matters of church order and organization. A man of strong views on many topics, Bates had the confidence of his brethren, who turned to him time after time to moderate conferences which were fraught with such serious consequences.

At this time the constituency of the Seventh-day Adventists numbered only 3,500, concentrated east of the Missouri River and north of the southern parallel of Missouri. There were about thirty ministerial workers at that time. But with organization effected, more rapid growth would be realized as the century progressed. Thus, in this phase of the church's progress, Joseph Bates also made his positive contribution.

15

A HEALTH REFORMER SHOWS THE WAY

(1863-1868)

Among the distinctive early features of the Seventh-day Adventist Church was the health reform emphasis, of which Joseph Bates was the personification. A temperance devotee back in the days before he became a Christian, a Millerite, or a Sabbatarian, he has provided us with a timetable of his re-nunciations of those things which he deemed were harmful to his physical being, and therefore in opposition to the will of God for him.

As early as 1821, at the height of his career as a successful seaman, he resolved never to drink another glass of ardent spirits. The following year he included wine in the resolve. He courageously held to this position, though he was under pressure at times to conform to the customs and practices of polite society on such matters as joining in toasts to prominent people.

Near the end of the following year he ceased using tobacco and put forth a great effort to eschew the use of profane language. As has been related, he helped organize the Fairhaven Temperance Society immediately after his baptism into the Christian Church in 1827.

In the early 1830's he abandoned the use of tea and coffee, and then ten years later, just before the expected great day of the Lord, he quit eating meat, butter, grease, cheese, pies, and rich cakes.

James White testified to the excellence of Bates's health in 1846, after some years of healthful practices: "When I first became acquainted with Elder Bates, he was fifty-four years of age. His countenance was fair, his eye was clear and mild, his figure was erect and of fine proportions, and he was the last man to be picked out of the crowd as one who had endured the hardships and exposure of sea life, and who had come in contact with the demoralizing influences of such a life for more than a score of years. It had been eighteen years since he left the seas, and during that time his life of rigid temperance in eating as well as in drinking, and his labors in the pure sphere of moral reform, had regenerated the entire man, body, soul, and spirit, until he seemed almost re-created for the special work to which God had called him."[1]

Despite his own rigid adherence to temperance principles in eating and drinking, Bates did not attempt to force his ideas on other people in his private contacts or public ministry. He did not stress these topics until after the church had embraced similar principles. After this, which came about in 1863, he and his fellow preachers often spoke on health reform as well as dress reform, in addition to the second advent and the Sabbath.

It is of no little significance that Bates, with his strict habits of food and drink, appears to have been relatively free from illness when his brethren, almost to a man, were incapacitated for longer or shorter periods of time. He simplified his diet for a time in 1845 to bread and water, and although induced to add to this fruits, nuts, and cereals, he retained water as his only drink.

His colleagues, Ellen and James White, Uriah Smith, Waggoner, Loughborough, Andrews, Bourdeau, and many others, suffered from health problems. But Bates, except for a brief period or two of "fever and ague," moved on, well deserving of the accolade as prime health reformer of the advent movement.

"Through thick and thin, sunshine and storm, in labors abundant and privations sore, he marched ever forward, serene above the physical troubles of his companions, ever sympathetic and helpful in their misfortunes, and never preaching except by his example, the doctrines of the health gospel.

"When in 1865 Andrews was sent into retirement by his ills, and Loughborough went along with him, Joseph Bates carried on. When James White, in 1865, was so sorely smitten with his most severe stroke of paralysis, when Loughborough almost immediately came into danger of the same disaster, when Uriah Smith, overcrowding his office labors and, because of his lameness wholly neglecting outdoor exercises, was invalided, when almost the whole personnel of the General Conference and its chief component, the Michigan Conference, were bundled off to the Dansville Sanitarium in New York, and the cause seemed about to sag into desuetude, Joseph Bates bore up the burden, cheering, working, and gathering funds from the Monterey church and elsewhere to send to the sufferers. And never did he point a self-righteous finger at himself or say, 'Live as I do, and you will not suffer so.' "[2]

It was indeed a sad group that left Battle Creek on September 14, 1865, to go to the Danville Sanitarium in New York. Among the party were James and Ellen White, John Loughborough, and Uriah Smith, accompanied by Dr. H. S. Lay.

"There went the president of the General Conference, one of his chief lieutenants, and the editor of the *Review and Herald*—all invalided. Other leaders were also in ill health. For nearly a year no quorum of either the General Conference Committee or the Michigan Conference Committee could be had, because of the illness of a majority."[3]

At this critical time Joseph Bates was virtually the only member who was consistently about his regular duties. In August, 1866, he again suffered from "fever and ague"; but he reported that water treatments and dieting cured him in three days.

As early as 1850 the attention of the advent believers had been called to the harmful effects of tea, coffee, and tobacco. Within ten years condemnation of these items was well-nigh unanimous among the believers.

In early June of 1863, in the critical summer of the Civil War which was hampering the work of evangelism, Ellen White, at Otsego, Michigan, received a vision of health reform in its wider aspects. Now attention was directed also to the superiority of "natural foods" over flesh food and the advantages healthwise of proper ventilation and proper clothing as well.

That year and the following, Ellen White's inspired thoughts on health were published and expanded with an immediate, hearty response from Seventh-day Adventists in general. Joseph Bates, who had stood almost alone for so long a time on the health question, now rejoiced to see such progress among the other church leaders, with the far-reaching results that followed.

From the outset the chief teachers of health and diet reform were moderate, sensible, and constructive. At its inception the health message was identified as an integral part of the religious teaching of the Seventh-day Adventist Church. Again the New Bedford sea captain, Joseph Bates, must be credited with contributing his influence in support of a prominent feature of the emerging Seventh-day Adventist Church.

One is struck with the candor with which the leaders of the early Adventist Church dealt with, and were dealt with by, their brethren. In their supreme quest for truth they even published and discussed ideas which seemed to have little merit or were erroneous. One illustration of this appears in a comment following an article submitted by Father Bates, as he now came to be called, and printed in the March 29, 1864, *Review*. In his article Bates applies Isaiah 30:8-10 to the prophecies of Daniel and the revelator.

After printing the article, apparently in its entirety, the editor added this disclaimer: "We are always glad to hear from our venerable Bro. Bates. It is evident that he loves the advent doctrine, and all connected with it that has been good. His application of the prophecy of Isaiah to the chart seems to us very apocryphal, but it will do no harm unless others make such doubtful exposition of equal importance with plainly revealed, vital points of doctrine."

The accounts of his travels which Bates furnished readers of the church journal indicate that he was involved in about 130 meeting days with the local Michigan churches during 1864. It would appear from his schedule that he was beginning to return to his home in Monterey oftener and staying there longer.

His reports suggest that he was oblivious to the war that was raging to its bloody and destructive close. Only very rarely does a reference indicate his awareness of the internecine conflict. In one report he reveals his complete sympathy with his section by referring to the conflict as "the rebellion." He also tells of some problems with members at Fair Plains, Michigan, who cannot get certificates from their church to establish their membership inasmuch as the church is not yet organized. He also mentions that some members from Hillsdale who had gone off to build bridges for the Government, faced problems, presumably involving Sabbath duties.

On election day, November 8, 1864, which saw Lincoln returned for a second term, Bates was in Brady, Michigan, where, because of the elections, not many people came out to hear him preach on the cardinal doctrines, and also on systematic benevolence and health and temperance themes.

Throughout most of the year 1865 Bates continued very actively to visit churches and hold meetings in his adopted state. Overtones of the continuing war appear from time to time in his reports. He states, for example, that the church in Monterey observed the call of the General Conference Committee to observe February 25 and March 1-4 as a time of fasting and prayer for (1) His precious suffering cause, (2) our bleeding country, and (3) the down trodden bondsmen.[4]

To illustrate his activities at this time, and for the last twenty years of his life in fact, his report to the editor of the *Review*, May 2, 1865, may be cited as a typical communication, one of several score appearing in the church paper after 1850 and almost right up until his death in 1872. He wrote:

"Brother White: We spent April 4th and 5th in Jackson, baptized one, and had a good meeting.

"April 6-9, a series of meetings in Tompkins, Jackson Co. Sabbath, the 8th inst., we enjoyed a season of refreshing while fasting and praying to the Lord to give power to the four angels [Rev. 7:2, 3] to stay the tide of the raging elements of political strife in our nation, and open the way for the downtrodden and oppressed bondmen to go free. In the providence of God, Brn. Newman of Windsor and Avery of Lock, had been thrown out of the draft at Jackson on account of disability, and Bro. N. was with us during the appointed fast. It was a day of joy and gladness. We felt that we were in union with all loyal people of God which had covenanted to keep the commandments of God and the faith of Jesus, and closed the day in celebrating the ordinances of the Lord's house.

"April 10th, enjoyed a refreshing social meeting with the church in Battle Creek. Their way, and work is onward. The Lord help us all to go forward in union and harmony is my prayer.

"The 11th and 12th, held two profitable meetings with the church in Newton, their numbers are increasing. Their neighbors manifested an interest to hear. I hope they will obey.

"From the 13th to the 17th, held six meetings with the church in Burlington. On the Sabbath the brethren from Newton united with us in celebrating the ordinances of the Lord's house, and were much refreshed and strengthened. A trial of some time standing was removed by humble confession and the brother received again into the bosom of the church. Two others were added to the church, and one baptized. The church is encouraged to press onward in the third angel's message.

"April the 18th and 19th, we were with the church in Hanover in Jackson Co. Here we held two meetings, the one on the 19th was appointed to convene at twelve o'clock at noon, in accordance with the appointment of Act. Sec. of State, to assemble to show our sympathies and respect for our noble-hearted, and much lamented Chief Magistrate, who was in such a desperate and sudden manner deprived of life, just as he (by, and under the direction of our merciful God,) was bringing to a peaceful close one of the most-unheard-of rebellions, and thereby liberating millions of his fellowmen from worse than Egyptian bondage. On account of the heavy storm, the meeting was thin; but those present manifested sympathy and respect.

"After this the church repaired to Bro. W. Carpenter's and celebrated the sufferings, and cruel death of our beloved Lord and Saviour Jesus Christ.

Joseph Bates

Hillsdale, Michigan, April 21, 1865."

Earlier this year he had reported a steady pace of traveling, preaching in places as far as forty miles from public transportation. The year 1865 also brought to Joseph Bates the sad news of his son's death at sea.

With the Civil War over and Lincoln in his grave in Springfield, Illinois, the struggle for power in the post-war Reconstruction period got under way in earnest. Evangelism was reviving after the handicaps imposed by the war. Bates reported an interest in his message by returning soldiers. He preached often now on the theme of systematic benevolence and dress and health reform. In March, 1866, he was in Battle Creek giving a stirring message on the Laodiceans, followed by testimonies by the people. As an indication of the progress of church organization, the conference assigned Bates to work in sixteen towns in the eastern portion of Michigan, and Byington in the western.

A little later the Michigan conference appointed Bates to the southern district for the second quarter of the year. His meetings in the town of Vassar led to a baptismal service in the Cass River where the banks, he reported, were lined on both sides with spectators. While in Jackson, Bates visited again in the home of D. R. Palmer, the first one to accept the Sabbath as the result of his ministry in Michigan in 1849.

Throughout his reports Bates referred to cases of healing by prayer during his ministry. In the spring of 1866 he mentioned a man who was healed of consumption at Wright, Michigan. At Greenbush he found a great interest in health reform, partly because of the healing of a little child who had been covered with sores. This was accomplished, he asserted, by the use of Graham pudding alone.

While in the vicinity of Flint, Michigan, Bates stopped to renew his acquaintance and to dine with Governor W. H. Crapo of Michigan. One might wonder about the contacts a penniless itinerant preacher might have with the chief officer of the state. However, Governor Crapo had grown up in New Bedford about the time Bates was a young man there. Crapo moved to Michigan in 1856, just two years before Bates. Crapo revealed unusual qualities which took him rapidly up the political ladder. He served two terms as governor. Bates, no doubt, nothing daunted because of his friend's high position, was concerned about the spiritual needs of the governor.

The General Conference met in the session of 1867 at Allegan, near Monterey, from June 1 to 3. The Allegan church had prepared with periods of fasting and prayer for the success of the general meetings. The record indicates that believers celebrated the ordinances, including foot washing, at Allegan in the spring.

The early Adventists debated among themselves the obligation of the Christian to celebrate the ordinance of foot washing periodically.[5] Supporters of the ordinance interpreted literally Christ's admonition to wash one another's feet. Those who opposed it linked foot washing (and the holy kiss, with which it was concluded) with fanaticism. Some precedents existed.

Ellen White counseled moderation on this question at first; but she soon endorsed the ordinance of humility, and it has come to be practiced just before the Lord's Supper on a quarterly basis. Bates seems to have celebrated these ordinances with the believers on many occasions as he traveled about in his ministry, often on the evening after the Sabbath.

Bates's liberality to the church and to those less fortunate than he, did not diminish with the passing of the years. He apparently had invested a little to help the Battle Creek Reform Institute to get on its feet. "Whatever amount of dividends growing out of this stock I hold in the Health Reform Institute of Battle Creek," he wrote, "is come to me, I wish the directors to apply to the charitable fund until otherwise directed."[6]

That he had not flinched or failed in his dietary position is shown by his report of a gathering in Holly on July 4, 1867, when "we all united and partook of a rich repast of the bounties of heaven furnished from the herb bearing seed and the fruit of the tree."[7]

Bates's name attracted from long distances people who were impressed by his messages as he worked on in his seventy-fifth year. Two sisters walked through the woods a distance of five miles to hear him preach on dress and health reform, then they retraced their steps the five miles to their homes after nine o'clock at night. Later one family came fifty miles from Ohio to his meetings at Ransom Center, Michigan, this in a day of limited travel conveniences. He expressed pleasure in the meetings held at his home church in Monterey in early September, conducted by Elder Loughborough and James and Ellen White. He felt the meetings were a success as measured by "hearing ears and falling tears."

Reports from Bates in 1868 do not indicate the extensive activity and travel which had been characteristic of him during previous years. Especially is this true of the first three fourths of the year, till the time of the first Seventh-day Adventist camp meeting at Wright, Michigan, from September 1 to 7 of that year. He mentions the almost incessant snowstorms which kept him at home during the early months of the year. The members in Monterey and Allegan were busily engaged in studying the *Testimonies* on dress and health reform, and in this study they received his attention.

Early in May, James and Ellen White worked with the Monterey Church and kept in close touch with Joseph and Prudence Bates, taking meals with them on several occasions. Mrs. White reported on the spirit of the church at Monterey in these words: "We never before witnessed such a work in Monterey in so short a time. First day fifty came forward for prayers. Brethren felt keenly for the lost sheep, and confessed their coldness and indifference, and took a good stand. Fourteen were baptized. The work moved on with solemnity, confessions, and much weeping, carrying all before it."[8]

In the summer of 1868 Bates wrote to his older sister, Harriot, a letter written partly to dispel rumors that had reached her of their being in want. "In other words," he wrote, "all our necessary wants are supplied. Our living is hygienic, the best grains, fruit, and vegetables the land offers." Regarding seeing this sister again he said, "I expect to see New England once more before it's lain [*sic*] in ruins." He mentions his life sketch, published this year in book form, and he says of his younger brother Franklin, "I send Franklin the *Review* and sent him my book."

His concluding sentence is in character, "I do really want to help you see the precious truths of the advent doctrines."[9]

In 1868 the first Adventist "missionaries" journeyed to the Pacific Coast. The year also witnessed the first Seventh-day Adventist camp meeting, held at Wright, Michigan, September 1 to 7, 1868.

"There were nineteen tents from churches in Michigan, one from Olcott, N.Y., and one each from Oakland and Johnstown, Wisconsin, making in all twenty-two tents on the ground, besides the Ohio and Michigan large meeting tents, each sixty feet in diameter. These, arranged in a circle around a preachers' stand, and the seats for the people, in the edge of the beautiful grove, made it a most pleasant and inviting spot."[10]

The following graphic description of an early Seventh-day Adventist camp meeting captures the spirit of the annual seasons of spiritual refreshing.

"The tents, which were of various sizes according to the number of persons to be accommodated, were mostly constructed with side walls of rough boards, the roof and ends being of factory cotton. The two large tents near the center were used for services only in case of rain, the speakers' stand

and the great majority of the seats being under the trees outside. The seats were of rough boards laid on logs, arranged longitudinally end to end. Logs alone were also used for seats. The rostrum, which stood out in the open, measured about ten by twelve feet, and was provided with a canopy. The camp was lighted at night by means of a number of wood fires which were kept burning on elevated boxes filled with earth. For the comfort of the campers in wet or chilly weather, a log fire was kept burning in the out-skirts. There was no grocery stand. Food was prepared in the farmhouses nearby, and brought warm to the camp. Bread wagons drove in from Berlin, the nearest village. . . .

"Among the prominent truths presented were the facts concerning the investigative judgment, and the need of a special preparation in order to stand before the throne of God."[11]

Speakers at the first camp meeting at Wright, Michigan, included Joseph Bates, James and Ellen White, J. N. Andrews, and J. H. Waggoner. The camp was supervised by White and Andrews, and at the meetings Bates recommended James White's book *Life Incidents* which had just come out. He refers also to people at the meeting who were on "anxious seats."

As has been noted, after a degree of urging by his friends, Joseph Bates consented to write out his life's sketch for the *Youth's Instructor*, then the denomination's weekly paper for its young people. These chapters concerned mainly his life at sea and went up to about 1840, with a brief sketch of the advent movement in the 1840's. This series ran for over five years in the *Instructor*, and a demand developed later for the articles in book form.

In 1868 the book appeared, and James White in announcing its availability in the *Review* described it in these words: "This is . . . one of the most inter-esting books in our country. . . . It is one of the best books in the world. . . . It should be in every family. The old friends of Father Bates should all take a special interest in this book. We have all been blest with the labors of this good man. Let none be too stingy to purchase a copy of his good book. When the printer and binder are paid, what remains from the sale of the book will go for the benefit of this pioneer of the cause, whom we all love. For sale at the Review Office, price $1. . . . Turn out some of those worthless books from the library, and let good ones take their places."[12]

The popularity of this book was such that within a decade of the death of Bates a new edition was published, edited by his companion in spiritual battles, James White. This life sketch comprises a main source of information on his life up to the early 1840's.

16

"HOME IS THE SAILOR"

(1868-1872)

All during the year 1869 Bates was out and about the "King's business." His diary for that year tells us that he was active at or near his home during January, as follows:

January 2, preaching, meetings in Monterey.

January 5, writing report of meetings, home duties, social meetings.

January 7, writing and visiting.

January 13, preparing wood and reading *Testimonies*.

January 14, visiting house to house and reading the *Testimonies*.

January 18, part of the day writing, part of the day working for self.[1]

And so his days went, until he felt impelled to take to the road again and minister to the needs of the churches.

By early spring he was in Jackson, Michigan, scene of his first labors in the state, twenty years before. While here he sought to meet with prisoners in the state penitentiary but was refused permission. Here also he met a sailor-preacher of the Methodist Episcopal Church who, like Bates, had sailed out of New Bedford. He also met his former pastor, Daniel Millard, whom he mentions in his autobiography. So he pushed on with optimism and vigor, giving out tracts in railroad cars and along the plank roads he traveled.[2]

Later this year he visited several Negroes in Fremont, where he had visited sixteen years before. At York Station he met an aged woman who had observed the seventh-day Sabbath for sixty-nine years. In late May he attended the annual session of the General Conference at Battle Creek.

Before making his final foray of the year 1869, which took him into Ohio, Bates wrote a lengthy defense of James and Ellen White, this in reply to a printed request by Andrews, Bell, and Smith. Published in the *Review,* it vindicated the Whites against certain charges made against them and attacks on their character. Bates said he had known James White since the autumn of 1845, and that he had worked closely with him for many years.[3] "It gives me," he wrote, "great pleasure to say that I have entire confidence in his honesty and uprightness." He further revealed that "he [White] has most generously donated from his own means to help sustain me in the work. As one instance I will mention the fact that at one time he furnished me with a house for my family for fourteen months, for which he refused to receive rent."[4] In 1863 Bates had similarly testified to the honesty and uprightness of James White in business dealings.[5]

The census of 1870 (June 27, 1870) listed Joseph Bates as a member of the clergy, SDA, aged seventy-seven. The value of his real estate was now listed as $1,000, and of personal possessions, $400. Prudence, his wife, was listed as aged seventy-seven. Also the Bateses' youngest daughter, Mary Reardon, was living with her parents, caring for them at this time. Her twelve-year-old son Willie resided with them.

Three days after Bates had interrupted one of his journeys to return home, his companion of fifty-two years passed to her rest on August 27, 1870. In her last letter to her husband shortly before, she had expressed a longing to have her mind free from care and household chores so that "I might more exclusively give my mind and time to the all-important subject of getting just right before the Lord."[6] Bates was not one to carry his feelings on his sleeve. "Beneath his iron self-control and behind his consuming passion for the cause, and despite his public indifference to family pride and social ties, the heart of Joseph Bates was tender and true. . . . After his wife died, he halted not at all, it would appear from his reports, only occasionally resting at his home as before."[7]

Within a few weeks after the funeral of his wife, Joseph Bates attended a camp meeting at Charlotte, where nearly a thousand Adventists were present, with the Whites doing most of the speaking.

Although earlier in his career Bates was skeptical of visions and similar manifestations, in later life he seems to have placed great significance on dreams and their meaning. In 1870 he set forth some of his dreams and his interpretations of them. One told of two birds flying about and being shot at by people, but the birds were not injured. This he applied to attacks on

James and Ellen White. Another dream concerned a wall with a ragged hole in it, which he said represented the publishing work. Another dream dealt with deep plowing and hard soil that could not be broken easily, and another with a flower bed which had significance, he said, for the Battle Creek Health Institute.⁸ Till the end, all his conscious thoughts seem to have been employed in his ministry. Is it any wonder that even his dreams were interpreted by him in the light of his consuming commitment?

The record of Bates's travels and preaching, as reflected in his reports to the church journal, does not support what might be our natural assumption that in his last years of life he slackened his pace appreciably.

On the contrary, it would seem that his desire to hasten the day of Christ's coming and reunion with his fallen companion spurred him on more than ever. In his letter he reports meetings and visits to churches every month until December. These occurred mainly in western and central Michigan, but in late summer he spent almost two weeks in northern Indiana. The pace of his work can be seen in the number of meetings he held—eight meetings in Alma in six days, five meetings in Pottersville in two days, and six meetings in Leighton, where he stayed only two days. Also at Pottersville he missed no opportunities with people he found "sitting in and around the railroad station house." These he found interested in what he had to say.

In the eleven months of 1871 when he was actively itinerating, he held at least a hundred meetings besides those in the local church and in addition to the conferences which he attended. His references to new meetinghouses encountered are frequent, and he speaks of them with approbation. He suggests the antiquity of an unfortunate term still used by some when he says that at Matherton "outsiders" attended. In Greenville he met with Danish brethren; and at Salem, Indiana, he revived the faith and courage of Sabbath keepers he had instructed sixteen years before.

Early in the year he attended the annual anniversary meeting at Battle Creek and found it "cheering to be associated with the brethren." Again in midsummer he was in Battle Creek for a health convention. It was at this meeting that he gave a moving testimony of his experience in putting away harmful food and drink and becoming thoroughly committed to the health-reform program. He also gave an indication of the state of his health at this time when he was seventy-nine years of age. He said, "Contrary to my former convictions, that if I was ever permitted to live to my present age, I should be a suffering cripple from my early exposure in following the sea, thanks be to God and our dear Lord and Saviour, whose rich blessing ever follows every personal effort to reform, that I am entirely free from aches and pains, with a gladdening, cheering prospect that if I continue to reform, and forsake every wrong, I shall, with the redeemed followers of the Lamb, stand 'without fault before the throne of God.' " Then follows this comment by Elder James White: "He then stood as straight as a monument, and would tread the sidewalks as lightly as a fox."[9]

The fourth annual camp meeting held at Charlotte in September, 1871, Bates felt, revealed a "deeper feeling never before witnessed." There were fifty-two tents pitched at this meeting, and nearly eight hundred Sabbath keepers present. Bates was one of the speakers at this session. Back in Monterey in November he reported that an epidemic of whooping cough was so bad that the schools and Sabbath Schools had been suspended for weeks.

After November, 1871, the familiar by-line of Joseph Bates, seen regularly in the *Review* since its inception in 1850, can no longer be found. However, as late as mid-February of 1872 he was still active enough to write a spirited letter to Ellen White defending his dietary practices from the charge of fanaticism. In this letter he explains the background of the report, which had grown out of all proportion, that he always asked God to bless only the clean food on the table. He actually had done this once at an out-of-door Fourth-of-July picnic of the church at Vassar.

This single episode he explained in his letter to Mrs. White in this way: "The tables were soon up and loaded with tempting eatables; and I was invited to ask the blessing. The swine's flesh upon the table, I knew was abominable and unclean from creation, . . . and God had positively, by law, forbidden the eating or touching of it. . . . I therefore very quietly distinguished, and asked a blessing on the clean, nutritious, wholesome, *lawful* food. Some whispered, and some smiled, and others looked, and so on."[10]

Elder Bates proceeded in his letter to Mrs. White to deal with the report that he and his daughter and her son were starving. He then listed all of their food supplies—an ample stock by any standard—all foods in keeping with his principles of natural, nutritious products of the field and tree.

A month after writing this letter Joseph Bates died, on March 19, 1872, at the Health Institute in Battle Creek. The cause of death was listed as putrid erysipelas and diabetes, which in our time would be subject to more precise diagnosis or explanation. He was buried at Poplar Hill Cemetery in Monterey, where almost one hundred of his Adventist brethren also rest. The original stone marking the resting-place of Joseph and Prudence Bates carried a brief sketch of his eventful life. His obituary states:

Joseph Bates in his later years.

This new headstone marks the graves of Joseph (1792-1872)
and Prudence (1793-1870) Bates in Monterey, Michigan.

"His last hours, though characterized by pain such as few men have been called upon to pass through, afforded a marked evidence of the superiority of a faith in Christ over the bodily suffering and the prospect of certain and rapidly approaching death. Having in early manhood chosen the service of God, and having for many years faithfully endeavored to live the life of the righteous, his last end was such as those alone can expect who have sedulously endeavored to preserve a conscience void of offense toward God and man."[11]

At the first convenient occasion after this, the Michigan Conference of Seventh-day Adventists passed the following resolution:

"That, as a tribute of respect, we recognize the decease of our beloved brother, Elder Joseph Bates, the loss of a great and good man, eminent for piety and Christian virtue; a pioneer in the third angel's message, always at his post of duty. We miss him in our assemblies, at our conference, in our churches, at our fireside homes; and while we deeply mourn our loss, we will remember his counsels, imitate his virtues, and endeavor to meet him in the kingdom of God."[12]

It would be almost presumptuous even to try to evaluate and summarize the vast contributions made by Joseph Bates to the early development and progress of the Seventh-day Adventist Church. His direct personal ministry led to the acceptance, by large numbers, of the second advent and Sabbath teaching. His indirect influence and efforts brought many more to the church. He was a trailblazer, opening up new areas, such as Michigan, a dozen years or so after it had achieved statehood. He pioneered the work in many centers, including Battle Creek, which for so long served as the headquarters of the church. He was the first Adventist Sabbatarian preacher in several states, including Wisconsin, Iowa, and Minnesota.

He contributed to the definition of Adventist doctrine, and although not always correct the first time, he was humble and teachable to the extent of accepting counsel from his fellow workers. One of his successors wrote of him that "one of the strongest traits of Joseph Bates was that he could receive help and even correction from his brethren."[13] In the category of theological positions which he modified might be mentioned the "shut door," the time for beginning and ending the Sabbath, setting a specific time for Christ to come, to mention just a few. Nevertheless, his contribution in clarifying points of doctrine was considerable.

His service as chairman of many meetings during the organizational period of the church was noteworthy. Also his bringing into the church so many who became great leaders must not be overlooked. Any partial list of such would include the names of S. N. Haskell, M. E. Cornell, John Byington, Annie Smith, R. F. Cottrell, and many more. Over and beyond all of the accomplishments of Joseph Bates along these lines, we must credit the confidence in the faith he inspired in his contemporaries and in those who have caught the inspiration of his life and service in the century since his death. His integrity, his total dedication to God and his fellows, and his Christlike demeanor would lead all who today are a part of the church which he helped to found to thank God for the heritage that he represents.

Thus ended the earthly career of a valiant, indefatigable, and unswerving apostle of Christ, outrider of the Apocalypse. These pages have sought to convey some idea of his work, his personality, and his achievements, particularly as a chief founder of the Seventh-day Adventist Church. Those whose lives he touched were impressed with his innate kindness and with the Christlike spirit which he consistently manifested.

"We see in him the daring, resourceful, imperious soul, self-disciplined, and schooled to the charity, meekness, and teachableness, of a Christian leader, yet with no loss of initiative, enterprise and power. . . .

"He was an exemplar of the ethics of social life. He was pioneer in the reform of diet and health habits. His personal example in eating, drinking, and all other relations told for much in building a foundation for that doctrine of health which has become a marked feature of the church he helped to found."[14]

One comes away from following all the available details of the life of

Joseph Bates with a great admiration for his sterling character, his single-minded devotion to the course he believed to be right, and the wide influence which he exerted while he lived and which even today he exerts while he sleeps. Truly he was a seasoned man for all seasons. He lived and died cherishing the "blessed hope."

And so, Joseph Bates—mariner, reformer, preacher—"gave his body to that pleasant country's earth." He had committed his life without reservation to his leader, Christ, "under whose colors he had fought so long."

JOSEPH BATES
(1792-1872)

Genealogical Chart

CLEMENT BATE   baptized 1594/5 -   in England
married Ann   to America with wife &
five children on *Elizabeth,*
Apr. 17, 1635.
died 1671   Name goes back to Lydd,
England, records. Bates
Society has copy of his will.

SAMUEL   baptized 1639
married Lydia Lapham of Scituate, 1666-7
died 1713

SAMUEL   born 1679-80
married Margaret Churchill* 1706. d. 1764
died 1730

BARNABAS   born 1718-19 at Wareham
married Phoebe Gibbs (1727-1816)
died 1795

JOSEPH BATES, SR.   born 1750 at Wareham (second eldest of 13)
married Deborah Nye of Sandwich 1784
died 1828

JOSEPH BATES, JR.   born 1792 (fourth child of seven)
married Prudence Nye, 1818 (1793-1870)
died 1872 at Monterey, Michigan

*of Mayflower ancestry

From "The Bates Bulletin," Vols. 1-5,
third series, 1917-22; and "Descendants of Clement Bate," pp. 23ff.
New York Public Library, Genealogy Room.

Chart · 121

MAP

OF THE

SURVEYED PART

OF

MICHIGAN,

BY

JOHN FARMER.

PUBLISHED BY J.H.COLTON.

NEW-YORK.

1855.

Engraved by S.Stiles & Co. New-York.

REFERENCES

Towns	Niles
County Seats	●
Villages	●●
Roads	
Rail Roads	
Canals	

NOTES AND REFERENCES

Chapter 1

1. Joseph Bates, Letter to Mrs. Bourne, 1868.
2. Samuel E. Morison, *The Maritime History of Massachusetts, 1783-1860,* page 314.
3. *Children's Story of New Bedford.*
4. Morison, *op. cit.,* p. 316.
5. Hegarty, Melville Whaling Room, New Bedford Free Public Library.
6. *Whale Fisheries of New England,* page 25.
7. Charles A. Harris, *Old Fairhaven,* Vol. 3, p. 121.
8. Although there is some uncertainty in identifying Joseph Bates's birthplace and other of his homes in his early years, there seems to be no question about the authenticity of the Meadow Farm residence. In 1886 the editor of the *Review and Herald* refers to a visit he made to the house and room where Joseph Bates was born, in Fairhaven, which he mistakenly described as "the birthplace of our cause."—*Review and Herald,* August 31, 1886.

Chapter 2

1. Joseph Bates, *Autobiography,* 1868 ed., pages 20-26. (Unless otherwise indicated, all references to the Bates *Autobiography* are to the 1868 edition.)
2. Cited in Morison, *Maritime History,* page 111.
3. Bates, *op. cit.,* p. 29.
4. "During the three or four years preceding the War of 1812 there were at least from 750 to 1,000 American seamen impressed annually."—James F. Zimmerman, *Impressment of American Seamen,* page 256.

Chapter 3

1. General entry book of American prisoners of war at Dartmoor Prison. Public Records Office, London, ADM 103, No. 89.
2. Bates, *Autobiography,* page 72.
3. Andrews, *Dartmoor,* quoted in Ellis, *History of New Bedford and Its Vicinity, 1802-1892,* pages 197 ff.
4. *Ibid.*
5. *Ibid.,* p. 201.
6. Ford (ed.), *Writings of J. Q. Adams,* 1814-1816, Vol. 5, p. 322.
7. New Bedford *Mercury,* July 7, 1815.
8. The next year an epoch ended when the last prisoner of war walked out through the gates. For thirty-four years, until 1850, the prison remained closed, and the great lowering buildings, scene of so much misery and heartache, became only a bad dream to those who escaped to tell its sordid story.

Chapter 4

1. Bristol County Northern District, Land Records. Duplicates on file at New Bedford Office of Register of Deeds.
2. James White, *Life of Bates,* page 116.

Chapter 5

1. The Melville Whaling Room in the Free Public Library in New Bedford, Massachusetts, contains a wealth of information about whaling in the period but also about

other aspects of maritime life such as ship logs, journals, voyage abstracts, pictures, and other valuable materials. The curator, Reginald B. Hegarty, is in love with his subject and radiates the thrill of the great maritime years of New Bedford.

2. Bates, *Autobiography,* page 180.

3. *Ibid.,* p. 185.

4. Permission to quote portions of the logbook of Captain Bates has been granted by Richard C. Kulgar, director, Old Portsmouth Historical Society Whaling Museum, New Bedford, Massachusetts.

Chapter 6

1. H. S. Commager (ed.), *Era of Reform 1830-1860,* page 7.

2. Quoted in *ibid.,* pp. 24, 25.

3. A curious letter recently came to light written by Bartholomew Taber to Joseph Bates, dated June 13, 1831, which suggests another activity of the retired sea captain at this period. It appears that a legitimate business for even a confirmed temperance advocate was the handling of spiritous liquors for medicinal purposes. This letter from an associate of Bates in this venture indicates that Tabor became agitated by Bates's tender conscience over the correctness of this arrangement. Bates's erstwhile associate in this activity testified to his basic integrity when he wrote, "I must say of you, sir, with all your profession of religion and amiable moral qualities both by precept and example, (all of which I revere and esteem)," yet having said this, he returns to the problem at issue between them, which was a difference of opinion over the correctness and in fact the legality of their activities in this area. The original letter is in the possession of George H. Taber of Pittsburgh, Pennsylvania, great-great-grandson of Joseph Bates.

4. Bates, *Autobiography,* page 236.

5. *Ibid.,* p. 242.

6. Office of the Register of Deeds, New Bedford, Massachusetts.

Chapter 7

1. H. A. Larrabee, "Trumpeter of Doomsday," *American Heritage,* April, 1964, page 100.

2. Quoted in Bates, *Autobiography,* page 249.

3. Jerome L. Clark, *1844,* Vol. 1, p. 39.

4. Quoted in Olsen, *Origin and Progress of Seventh-day Adventists,* page 130.

5. B. A. Weisberger, "Pentecost in the Back Woods," *American Heritage,* June, 1959, page 81.

6. Bates, *Autobiography,* page 266.

7. Harris, *Fairhaven,* Vol. 1, p. 128.

8. Letter in E. G. White Estate, Washington, D.C.

9. Bates, *op. cit.,* p. 279.

10. *Ibid.,* p. 283.

Chapter 8

1. Bates, *Autobiography,* page 298.

2. "The Experiences of Former Days, No. 3," *Review and Herald,* August 11, 1904.

3. *Review and Herald,* Aug. 16, 1923.

4. *Ibid.*

5. L. E. Froom, *Prophetic Faith of Our Fathers,* Vol. 4, p. 833.

Chapter 9

1. Arthur W. Spalding, *Origin and History of Seventh-day Adventists,* Vol. 1, p. 155.

2. Joseph Bates, *The Seventh Day Sabbath, A Perpetual Sign.* (A portion of the desk on which this tract was written has been preserved and is now on display at Union College in Lincoln, Nebraska.)

3. Ellen G. White (compiler), *Life Sketches,* page 98.

4. Joseph Bates, *A Seal of the Living God,* page 24.

5. White, *op. cit.,* pp. 112, 113.

6. Arthur W. Spalding, *Captains of the Host,* page 227, 228.

7. *Ibid.,* p. 269.

8. E. G. White Diaries, MS 7, 1873.

9. These pamphlets, and certain other materials, are in the Advent Source Collection in the General Conference of Seventh-day Adventists, in Washington, D.C. Copies have been given to the Loma Linda University library through the kindness of the E. G. White Trustees, and particularly Arthur L. White, secretary of this organization. Permission to publish material from the unpublished diaries and letters of Ellen White has been granted to the author by the trustees of the Ellen G. White Estate.

10. Bates, Letter to Brother and Sister Hastings, written seventeen miles from Bangor, Maine.

Chapter 10

1. S. E. Morison and H. S. Commager, *The Growth of the American Republic,* 6th ed., Vol. 1, p. 568.

2. John Greenleaf Whittier, *Anti-slavery Poems.*

3. Bates, *Review and Herald,* Dec., 1850.

4. Arthur W. Spalding, *Footprints of the Pioneers,* page 117; Spalding, *Origin and History,* Vol. 1, p. 271.

5. Bates, *Review and Herald,* March, 1851.

6. R. V. Harlow, *Gerrit Smith: Philanthropist and Reformer,* page 214.

Gerrit Smith had also been sympathetic to the Millerites. On the eve of the October 22, 1844, expectation he wrote to his wife that even if their calculations should prove untrue "their endeavors have sprung from their loving hearts—their mistakes in calculations but from their heads." He regretted that he had taken "so little account of them." He also regretted that he and his wife were apart just at this time, for it might be the last evening before eternity. Then he added, "Perhaps [this] is the last evening of time."—Gerrit Smith Papers, C. S. Miller Collection, Syracuse University, Syracuse, New York.

7. Bates, Letter, Jan. 16, 1852.

8. Quoted in A. L. White, *Prophetic Guidance,* page 25.

9. Ellen G. White Diaries and Letters, MS 12, 1850.

10. Quoted in Spalding, *Captains of the Host,* page 182.

11. Ellen G. White, Letters and Diaries, MS 14, 1850; MS 11, 1850; letter to Brother Hastings, March 18, 1850. B-2-52, June 2, 1852.

12. *Review and Herald,* November, 1850.

13. *Advent Herald,* May 4, 1850, quoted in *Review and Herald,* Nov., 1850.

14. *Review and Herald,* July 23, 1853.

15. *Ibid.,* Dec. 23, 1851.

16. *Ibid.,* Aug. 6, 1857.

Chapter 11

1. *Review and Herald,* March 23, 1852.

2. E. N. Dick, *The Founders of the Message,* page 146.

3. J. O. Corliss, "Experiences of Former Days, No. 9," *Review and Herald,* Sept. 22, 1904.

Chapter 12

1. Tradition associates Bates with responsibility for starting the work of Seventh-day Adventists in various lands by means of tracts and papers placed on ships, but none of these specific claims have been authenticated to date.

2. *Review and Herald,* Aug. 28, Sept. 4, 11, and 18, 1856.

3. *Ibid.,* Feb. 21, 1856.

4. *Ibid.,* Feb. 19, 1857.

5. Olsen, *Origin and Progress of SDA,* pages 227, 228.

6. *Review and Herald,* Oct. 29, 1857.

7. *Ibid.,* Nov. 12, 1857.

Chapter 13

1. E. G. White, *Testimonies for the Church,* Vol. 1, pp. 146, 147, 148, 149.

2. *Review and Herald,* Jan. 23, 1919.

3. E. G. White, Diaries and Letters, MS 4, 1860.

4. Quoted by Bert Van Horn in "Early History of the Church at Monterey, Mich.," *Review and Herald,* Jan. 23, 1919.

5. *Ibid.,* May 31, 1870.

6. Original letter in possession of R. R. Bietz, vice-president of the General Conference of SDA.

7. Ellen White Diary entry, Feb. 4, 1859.

8. *Review and Herald,* May 26, 1859.

9. *Ibid.,* June 9, 1859.

10. *Ibid.,* Nov. 30, 1859.

Chapter 14

1. *Seventh-day Adventist Encyclopedia,* art. "Marion Party," page 754.

2. *Review and Herald,* Oct. 16, 23, 1860.

3. *Ibid.,* Aug. 16, 1923.

4. Arthur W. Spalding, *Captains of the Host,* page 246.

5. *Review and Herald,* April 30, 1861.

6. *Ibid.,* June 10, 1862.

7. "Following the Pioneers in Historic Michigan," E. G. White Publications.

8. E. G. White, Letters and Diaries, MSS 13, 14, 15, 1864 (Battle Creek).

9. Spalding, *op. cit.* p. 273.

Chapter 15

1. James and Ellen G. White, *Christian Temperance and Bible Hygiene,* page 252, 253, quoted in Olsen, *Origin and Progress,* page 259.

2. Arthur W. Spalding, *Footprints of the Pioneers,* page 167.

3. Spalding, *Captains of the Host,* page 323.

4. *Review and Herald,* March 21, 1865.

5. C. O. Smith, "An Inquiry Into the History and Significance of the Rite of Feet-

washing in the Christian Church."
6. *Review and Herald,* July 9, 1867.
7. *Ibid.,* Aug. 6, 1867.
About this time J. N. Loughborough's wife died. He held meetings at Allegan, near Monterey, Michigan. His diary for Dec. 26, 1867, states: "Rose at 7¼. Breakfast at Brother Bates. Walked two miles."
8. E. G. White, *Life Sketches,* page 189.
9. Letter to Sister Harriot, written at Monterey, July 19, 1868.
10. *Review and Herald,* Sept. 15, 1868.
11. Olsen, *Origin and Progress,* pages 274, 275.
12. *Review and Herald,* Nov. 17, 1868.

Chapter 16

1. Joseph Bates's Diary, 1869.
2. *Review and Herald,* March 29, 1868.
3. Other reports indicate their first meeting occurred in 1846. "We first met Elder Bates at his home in Fairhaven, Massachusetts, in the year 1846."—James White, *Life of Bates,* pp. 310, 311.
4. *Defense of Elder James White and His Wife, A Vindication of Their Moral and Christian Character.* (New York Public Library.)
5. *Review and Herald,* April, 1863.
6. Quoted in Arthur W. Spalding, *Footprints of the Pioneers,* page 165.
7. *Ibid.,* p. 168.
8. Original copy in E. G. White Estate, Washington, D.C.
9. James White, *Life of Bates,* pages 315, 316.
10. *Ibid.,* p. 317.
11. *Ibid.,* p. 320.
12. *Ibid.*
13. W. A. Spicer, *Pioneers of the Advent Movement,* page 138.
14. Spalding, *Captains of the Host,* pages 42, 43.

BIBLIOGRAPHY

I. Original Manuscripts

Abstracts of whaling voyages, 1831-1873, Dennis Wood, compiler. Melville Whaling Room, Free Public Library, New Bedford, Massachusetts.

Account books of the whaling industry, New Bedford and Nantucket, Massachusetts, 1774-1922. Baker Library, Graduate School of Business Administration, Harvard University.

Joseph Bates's Diary for 1869. Andrews University Library.

Joseph Bates's King James Version of the Bible. Inscribed "My father's Bible, Mary Nye Reardon, 1913." Andrews University Library.

Joseph Bates. His hymnbook with notations. Andrews University Library.

Joseph Bates. Last will and testament. Allegan, Michigan, 1872.

Joseph Bates, Sr., of Fairhaven. Last will and testament on file at Taunton, Massachusetts, in the county of Bristol, approved July 29, 1828.

Catherine Byington Diaries. Andrews University Library.

General Entry Book of American Prisoners of War at Dartmoor Prison. Public Record Office, Chancery Lane, London. ADM, 103, 89, Prisoner 3195.

A general letter, Joseph Bates to the church in Monterey and Allegan, Michigan, n.d., but presumably written about 1857. Original in possession of R. R. Bietz, Vice-president, General Conference of SDA.

Letter from Bates to Leonard Hastings, New Ipswich, New Hampshire, April 25, 1858. Original in possession of granddaughter, Mildred Alvira Hastings, of New Ipswich, New Hampshire.

Bates to Mr. and Mrs. Leonard Hastings, August 7, 1848, from Fairhaven. (Any others mentioned of Bates except as noted are in the Ellen G. White Publications collection in Washington, D.C.)

To Mr. and Mrs. Hastings, September 25, 1849, from Joseph Bates, written from near Bangor, Maine.

Statement by Joseph Bates written in longhand late in 1867 recounting several dreams which he had had recently and suggesting their interpretation.

Letter from Bates to his sister, Harriot, Monterey, Michigan, July 19, 1868.

Joseph Bates to his older sister, Sophia Bourne, at Boston, written from Fairhaven, December 24, 1842.

Letter to Mr. and Mrs. Leonard Hastings of New Ipswich, New Hampshire, written by Joseph Bates from Fairhaven, April 7, 1848.

Letter to Ellen White from Bates, written at Monterey, February 14, 1872.

Letter from Ellen White to Joseph Bates written at Gorham, Maine, July 13, 1847. This original letter in the White Estate vaults in Washington is the oldest Ellen G. White letter in the White Estate vaults at the present time. She had married James White less than a year before this letter was written.

Letter to Joseph Bates from Bartholomew Taber dated June 13, 1831, at Fairhaven. The original in possession of the great-great-grandson of Joseph Bates, George H. Taber of Pittsburgh, Pennsylvania.

Land transactions. 1828-1844, recorded in Bristol County Registry of Deeds in Taunton and New Bedford, Massachusetts.

Log of the ship *Empress*, voyage of 1827-1828, Old Dartmouth Historical Society, Johnny Cake Hill, New Bedford, Massachusetts.

Loughborough, J. N., Diary. Andrews University, Berrien Springs, Michigan.

Manuscript Cartographic Items—maps, statistics, etc., 1850-1870. The Michigan Historical Commission Archives, Lansing, Michigan.

Papers of Henry Howland Crapo, 1804-1869. Michigan Historical Collection, University of Michigan.

Records of Fairhaven Academy, Coggeshall Memorial, Fairhaven, Massachusetts.

Records of the Seventh-day Adventist church, Monterey, Michigan, 1860-1872. Andrews University Library.

The Gerrit Smith papers. George Arents Research Library, Syracuse University.

The Ellen G. White Diaries and Letters, 1850-1873. Ellen G. White Publications, Washington, D.C.

II. Public Documents

American Agents for Seamen in Great Britain—William Lyman, 1805-1810. R. G. Beasley, 1810-1812.

The Annual United States Decennial Censuses, 1790-1870.

Bristol County, Northern District Land Records. County records at Taunton, Massachusetts.

Heads of families at the first census of the United States taken in the year 1790, Massachusetts. Washington: Government Printing Office, 1908, reprinted in 1964.

Historical data relating to counties, cities, and towns in Massachusetts. F. W. Cook, secretary to the commonwealth, 1948.

Index of marriages in Massachusetts Centinel and Columbian Centinel. 1784-1840, compiled by American Antiquarian Society. Boston: G. K. Hall, 1961.

Land records. Volume XXIV. New Bedford records office, New Bedford, Massachusetts.

Report of the Committee of the House of Representatives of Massachusetts on the Subject of Impressed Seamen: With the Evidence and Documents Accompanying It. Boston: Russell and Cutler, Printers, 1813.

Rochester, Massachusetts, vital records to 1850.

Soldiers and sailors in the American Revolution, Section V. The Institute of American Genealogy. Chicago, 1929.

Vital records of Barre, Massachusetts, to the end of the year 1949. Franklin P. Rice, Worcester, Massachusetts. 1963.

Vital records of Dartmouth, Massachusetts, to the year 1850. Vol. 3, Deaths. New England Historical and Genealogical Society, Boston, Massachusetts, 1930.

Vital records of New Brunswick, Massachusetts, to the year 1850. Vol. 1, Births; Vol. 2, Marriages; Vol. 3, Deaths. New England Historical and Genealogical Society, Boston, 1932.

Vital statistics of Fairhaven, Massachusetts, in the office of the City Clerk.

III. Pamphlets

Bates, Joseph. *An Explanation of the Typical and Antitypical Sanctuary, by the Scriptures.* New Bedford: Press of Benjamin Lindsay, 1850. 16 pages.

————. *A Seal of the Living God. A hundred forty-four thousand of the servants of God being sealed, in 1849.* New Bedford: Press of Benjamin Lindsay, 1849. 72 pages.

————. *Second Advent Waymarks and High Heaps, or a Connected View of the Ful-*

fillment of Prophecy, by God's Peculiar People From the Year 1840-1847. New Bedford: Press of Benjamin Lindsay, 1847. 80 pages.

_____. *The Opening of Heavens, or a Connected View of the Testimony of the Prophets and Apostles, Concerning the Opening Heavens, Compared With Astronomical Observations, and of the Present and Future Location of the New Jerusalem, the Paradise of God.* New Bedford: Press of Benjamin Lindsay, 1846. 40 pages.

_____. *The Seventh Day Sabbath, a Perpetual Sign, From the Beginning to the Entering Into the Gates of the Holy City, According to the Commandment.* New Bedford: Press of Benjamin Lindsay, 1846. 48 pages.

_____. *The Seventh Day Sabbath, a Perpetual Sign From the Beginning to the Entering Into the Gates of the Holy City, According to the Commandment.* New Bedford: Press of Benjamin Lindsay, 1847. Revised and enlarged to 63 pages.

_____. *A Vindication of the Seventh Day Sabbath With a Further History of God's Peculiar People From 1847-1848.* New Bedford, Massachusetts, 1848. 116 pages.

A Brief Sketch of the Origin, Progress and Principles of the Seventh-day Adventists. Edition of 1888. 46 pages.

Conradi, L. R. *The Founders of the Seventh-day Adventist Denomination.* Plainfield, New Jersey: American Sabbath Tract Society, 1939. 80 pages.

Defense of Elder James White and His Wife: A Vindication of Their Moral and Christian Character. Steam Press, Battle Creek, Michigan, 1870.

First Report of the General Conference of Christians Expecting the Advent of Our Lord Jesus Christ, held in Boston, October 14, 15, 1840. Boston: Joshua V. Himes, 1841.

Mutual Conference of Adventists at Albany, New York, 1845. The Peterson Advent Collection, New York Public Library. 32 pages.

Preble, P. M. *Tract, Showing That the Seventh Day Sabbath Should Be Observed as the Sabbath, Instead of the First Day.* Nashua, New Hampshire: Printed by Murray and Kimble, 1845. 12 pages.

Second Advent Tracts, No. 8. Proceedings of the Second Session of the General Conference of Christians Expecting the Advent of our Lord Jesus Christ, held in Lowell, Massachusetts, June 15, 16, 17, 1841.

A Word to the Little Flock. Notes by E. S. Ballenger. 34 pages.

Also various Millerite and Advent pamphlets, tracts, and papers in the Adventual Collection, Aurora College, Aurora, Illinois.

IV. Articles From Periodicals

Bates, Joseph. "Life Sketches," *Youth's Instructor,* 51 articles, 1858-1863. Later modified and printed in 1868 as his autobiography.

Series of articles in the *Review and Herald* by Bates:
November 10, 1850, "The Laodicean Church."
December, 1850, "New Testament Testimony."
December, 1850, "Midnight Cry in the Past."
January, 1851, "New Testament Seventh-day Sabbath."
January, 1851, "Duty to Our Children."
January, 1851, "Attitude in Prayer."
February, 1851, "The Weekly Sabbath."
April 7, 1851, "The Holy Sabbath."
April 21, 1851, "Time to Commence the Holy Sabbath."
August 5, 1851, "The Beast With Seven Heads."

August 19, 1851, "Our Labor in Philadelphia and Laodicean Churches."
June 24, 1852, "Seventh-day Sabbath Abolished."
February 17, 1853, "Thoughts on the Past Work of William Miller."
May 26, 1853, "Seventh-day Sabbath."
August 29, 1854, "Church Order."
September 12, 1854, "Nahum's Prophecy."
March, 1857, "Unlawful Marriages."
April 2, 1857, "Baptism."
May 12, 1859, pages 197 and 198.
In addition there were a number of articles appearing in the *Review and Herald* during the years after Joseph Bates's death dealing with recollections of some who were active in the early days of the work.

Brown, Ira V. "The Millerites and the Boston Press," *New England Quarterly,* December, 1943, pages 592-614.
————. "Watchers for the Second Coming: The Millennarian Tradition in America," *Mississippi Valley Historical Review,* December, 1952, pages 441-458.
Corliss, J. O. "The Experiences of Former Days," *Review and Herald,* Aug. 11, 1904; Sept. 22, 1904.
———— "The Message and Its Friends," *Review and Herald,* Aug. 16, 1923.
Emerson, Ralph Waldo. "Chardon Street and Bible Conventions," *The Dial,* July, 1842.
Horn, Jason. "Seventh-day Adventist Archives," *The American Archivist,* July, 1954, pages 221-224.
Johnson, Charles A. "The Frontier Camp Meeting: Contemporary and Historical Appraisals, 1805-1840," *Mississippi Valley Historical Review,* June, 1950.
Larrabee, Harold A. "The Trumpeter of Doomsday," *American Heritage,* April, 1964.
Loughborough, J. N. "The Second Advent Movement," *Review and Herald,* Aug. 18, 1921.
McAfee, Ida A. "New Bedford a Hundred and Twenty Years Ago as Glimpsed Through the Medley," *Proceedings of the 37th Meeting of the Old Dartmouth Historical Society,* January 29, 1913. New Bedford, Massachusetts, pages 5-24.
Van Horn, Bert. "Early History of the Church at Monterey, Mich.," *Review and Herald,* Jan. 23, 1919.
Weisberger, Bernard A. "Pentecost in the Backwoods," *American Heritage,* June, 1959.
White, Arthur L. "Divine Leadings in Early Days," *The Ministry,* August, 1941.
White, James. "Life Sketches of Joseph Bates," *Health Reformer,* January-February, 1877.

V. Newspapers and Periodicals

The Advent Harbinger, 1852.
Advent Herald, 1844.
The Battle Creek *Journal,* 1860's.
The Evening Standard, New Bedford, November, 1896.
The Midnight Cry, Joshua V. Himes, publisher, N. Southard, editor, New York, 1844.
The New Bedford *Mercury,* 1810-1815, 1818.
The New England Gazette, 1829.
The Present Truth, Middletown, Connecticut, 1849.
The Signs of the Times, Himes and Litch, editors, Boston, 1842.
The Tavistock *Times,* England, June 13, 20, 27, 1969.
In addition, incomplete files of various Adventist publications in the library of Berkshire Christian College, Lenox, Massachusetts.

VI. Books

Adams, Grayson Edward Hutter. *The Mad Forties.* New York: Harper and Brothers, 1942.

Andrews, Charles. *The Prisoner's Memoirs, or Dartmoor Prison.* New York: printed for the author, 1815.

Andross, Matilda Erickson. *The Story of the Advent Message.* Takoma Park, Washington, D.C.: Review and Herald Publishing Association, 1926.

Atholl, Justin. *Prisoner on the Moor; the Story of Dartmoor Prison.*

Bates, Joseph. *The Autobiography of Elder Joseph Bates.* Battle Creek, Michigan: Steam Press of the Seventh-day Adventist Publishing Association, 1868.

Bestor, Arthur E. *Backwoods Utopias. The Sectarian and Owenite Phases of the Communitarian Socialism in America: 1663-1829.* Philadelphia: University of Pennsylvania Press, 1950.

Billington, Ray A. *The Protestant Crusade, 1800-1860. A Study of the Origins of American Nativism.* New York: Macmillan, 1938.

Bliss, Sylvester. *Memoirs of William Miller Generally Known as a Lecturer on the Prophecies on the Second Coming of Christ.* Boston: J. V. Himes, Publisher, 1853.

Browne, Benjamin F. *The Yarn of a Yankee Privateer.* Nathaniel Hawthorne, ed. Funk & Wagnalls, 1926.

Buley, Roscoe C. *The Old Northwest, Pioneer Period, 1815-1840.* Bloomington: Indiana University Press, 2 volumes, 1951.

Clark, Elmer T. *The Small Sects in America.* Nashville: Cokesbury Press, 1937.

Clark, Jerome L. *1844.* 3 volumes. Nashville: Southern Publishing Association, 1968.

Commager, Henry Steele. *The Era of Reform, 1830-1860.* Princeton: D. Van Nostrand Company, Inc., 1960.

Cook, Norma P. *A Brief History of William Miller the Great Pioneer in Adventual Faith.* Boston: Advent Christian Publication Society, 1895.

Crisler, C. C., ed. *Life of Joseph Bates.* Takoma Park, Washington, D.C.: Review and Herald Publishing Association, 1927.

————. *Organization, Its Character and Purpose. Place and Development in the Seventh-day Adventist Church.* Takoma Park, Washington, D.C.: Review and Herald Publishing Association, 1938.

Dick, Everett N. *Founders of the Message.* Takoma Park, Washington, D.C.: Review and Herald Publishing Association, 1938.

Ellis, L. B. *History of New Bedford and Its Vicinity, 1602-1892.* Syracuse, New York: D. Mason and Company, 1892.

Fairhaven Old Home Week Association, *A Brief History of the Town of Fairhaven, Massachusetts.* Prepared in connection with the celebration of Old Home Week, July 26-31, 1903.

Ford, Worthington Chauncey, ed. *Writings of John Quincy Adams, Vol. 5, 1814-1816.* New York: The Macmillan Company, 1915.

Froom, L. E. *The Prophetic Faith of Our Fathers.* 4 volumes. Takoma Park, Washington, D.C.: Review and Herald Publishing Association, 1946-1954.

Cross, Whitney R. *The Burned Over District. Social and Intellectual History of Enthusiastic Religion in Western New York 1800-1850.* New York: Cornell University Press, 1950.

Harlow, Ralph Volney. *Gerrit Smith: Philanthropist and Reformer.* New York: Henry Holt and Company, 1939.

Harris, Charles A. *Old-Time Fairhaven.* 3 volumes, 1947-1954. New Bedford, Massachusetts: Reynolds Printing, 1947.

Hegarty, Reginald. *New Bedford's History*. Reynolds Printing Company, 1959.

History of Allegan and Barry Counties, Michigan. Philadelphia: D. W. Ensign and Company, 1880.

Howell, Emma E. *The Great Advent Movement*. Takoma Park, Washington, D.C.: Review and Herald Publishing Association, 1935.

Haskell, S. N. *The Pioneers and Leaders of a Mighty Movement*. (No facts of publication.) 32 pages.

Hudson, Winthrop S. *American Protestantism*. Chicago: University of Chicago Press, 1961.

Jenks, Ora. *William Miller and Early Phases of the Advent Movement*. Boston, 1832.

Johnson, Albert C. *Advent Christian History*. Boston: Advent Christian Publication Society, 1918.

Langley, Harold D. *Social Reform in the United States 1798-1862*. University of Illinois, 1967.

Life in New Bedford a Hundred Years Ago. Diary of Joseph R. Anthony, 1823-1824. Edited by Zephaniah W. Pease. Published by George H. Reynolds. Auspices of the Old Dartmouth Historical Society, 1922.

Loughborough, J. N. *The Church: Its Organization, Order and Discipline*. Washington, D.C.: Review and Herald, 1907.

————. *The Great Second Advent Movement: Its Rise and Progress*. Nashville: Southern Publishing Association, 1905.

————. *Rise and Progress of the Seventh-day Adventists*. Battle Creek: General Conference Association of Seventh-day Adventists, 1892.

Ludlum, David M. *Social Ferment in Vermont 1791-1850*. New York: Columbia University Press, 1939.

Miller, Perry. *The Life of the Mind in America From the Revolution to the Civil War*. New York: Harcourt, Brace and World, 1965.

Morison, S. E. *The Maritime History of Massachusetts, 1783-1860*. Boston: Houghton Mifflin, 1961.

Munger, Hiram. *Life and Religious Experience of Hiram Munger, etc*. Boston: Advent Christian Publication Society, 1881.

Nichol, Francis D. *The Midnight Cry*. Takoma Park, Washington, D.C.: Review and Herald Publishing Association, 1944.

Niebuhr, H. Richard. *The Social Sources of Denominationalism*. Cleveland: World, 1929.

Olsen, Mahlon Ellsworth. *A History of the Origin and Progress of Seventh-day Adventists*. Takoma Park, Washington, D.C.: Review and Herald Publishing Association, 1925.

Palmer, Benjamin F. *Diary of Benjamin F. Palmer, Privateersman, While a Prisoner on Board English Warships at Sea . . . and at Dartmoor*. Acorn Club of Connecticut, 1914.

Pease, Zephaniah W. *The Diary of Samuel Rodman: A New Bedford Chronicle of Thirty-seven Years, 1821-1857*. New Bedford: Reynolds Printing Co., 1927.

Reigel, R. E. *Young America 1830-1840*. Norman, Oklahoma: University of Oklahoma Press, 1949.

Representative Men and Old Families of Southeastern Massachusetts, Vol. 2. Chicago: J. H. Beers and Company, 1912.

Robinson, Dores Eugene. *The Story of Our Health Message*. Nashville: Southern Publishing Association, 1943.

Robinson, Ella M. *S. N. Haskell, Man of Action*. Review and Herald Publishing Association, Washington, D.C., 1967.

Robinson, Virgil E. *Cabin Boy to Advent Crusader*. Nashville: Southern Publishing Association, 1960.

Seventh-day Adventist Encyclopedia, Commentary Reference Series Volume 10, "Foot Washing," pages 414, 415; "Marion Party," page 754. Washington, D.C.: Review and Herald Publishing Association, 1966.

Ship Registers of New Bedford, Massachusetts. Vol. 2, 1851-1865. The National Archives Project, WPA, Boston, 1940.

Smith, Timothy L. *Religion in the Development of American Culture 1765-1840*. New York: Scribner's, 1952.

Spalding, Arthur Whitfield. *Footprints of the Pioneers*. Takoma Park, Washington, D.C.: Review and Herald, 1947.

_____. *Origin and History of Seventh-day Adventists*. 4 volumes. Washington, D.C.: Review and Herald Publishing Association, 1961.

_____. *Pioneer Stories of the Second Advent Movement*. Nashville, Tennessee: Southern Publishing Association, 1922.

Spicer, William A. *Pioneer Days of the Advent Movement, With Notes on Pioneer Workers and Early Experience*. Takoma Park, Washington, D.C.: Review and Herald, 1941.

Tullett, Tom. *Inside Dartmoor*. Muller, 1966.

Tyler, Alice F. *Freedom's Ferment: Phases of American Social History From the Colonial Period to the Outbreak of the Civil War*. New York: Harper and Row, 1962.

Wellcome, Isaac C. *History of the Second Advent Message and Mission, Doctrine and People*. Boston: Advent Christian Publication Society, 1874.

White, Ellen G., compiler. *Life Sketches of Ellen G. White*. Mountain View: Pacific Press Publishing Association, 1915.

White, James, ed. *The Early Life and Later Experience and Labors of Elder Joseph Bates*. Battle Creek: Steam Press of the SDA Publishing Association, 1878.

_____. *Life Incidents in Connection With the Great Advent Movement as Illustrated by the Three Angels of Revelation 14*. Battle Creek: Steam Press of the SDA Publishing Association, 1868.

_____. *Sketches of The Christian Life and Public Labors of William Miller*. Battle Creek: Steam Press of the SDA Publishing Association, 1875.

Zimmerman, James Fulton. *Impressment of American Seamen*. Port Washington, New York: Kennikat Press, reissued 1966.

VII. Unpublished Material

Arthur, David Talmage. "Joshua V. Himes and the Cause of Adventism 1839-1845." Unpublished M.A. thesis, University of Chicago, June, 1961.

Balharrie, Gordon. "A Study of the Contribution Made to the Seventh-day Adventist Movement by John Nevin Andrews." Unpublished M.A. thesis, Seventh-day Adventist Theological Seminary, Washington, D.C., 1949. 146 pages.

Dick, Everett N. "The Adventist Crisis of 1843-1844." Unpublished Ph.D. dissertation, University of Wisconsin, 1930.

Gane, Erwin Roy. "The Arian or Antitrinitarian Views Presented in Seventh-day Adventist Literature and the Ellen G. White Answer." Unpublished M.A. thesis, Andrews University, SDA Theological Seminary, June, 1963.

Hammond, Richard Julian. "Life and Work of Uriah Smith." Unpublished M.A.

thesis, Seventh-day Adventist Theological Seminary, Washington, D.C., 1949. 146 pp.

Harkness, Reuben E. "Social Origins of the Millerite Movement." Unpublished Ph.D. dissertation, University of Chicago, 1927.

Rojas, Billy. "The Origins of Millennial Speculation During the 1840's, the Background and Development of the Millerite Movement." Unpublished M.A. thesis, Roosevelt University, 1966.

Smith, Charles O. "An Inquiry Into the History and Significance of the Rite of Feetwashing in the Christian Church." Unpublished M.A. thesis, SDA Theological Seminary, Washington, D.C., August, 1940.

Stenberg, Clarence Edwin. "A Study of the Influence of Joseph Bates on the Denomination of Seventh-day Adventists." Unpublished M.A. thesis, SDA Theological Seminary, Washington, D.C., September, 1950. 108 pages.

VIII. Miscellaneous

"The Bates Association," newsletter in which may be traced the genealogy of Joseph Bates going back to his forebears in England in the sixteenth century. In the Genealogy Collection of New York City Public Library.

"Deaths" recorded in the New Bedford *Mercury,* 1807-1845.

"Deaths" recorded in the New Bedford *Mercury,* 1845-1874, Vol. 1.

"Marriages" copied from the New Bedford *Mercury,* 1807-1845, New Brunswick, 1912.

"Marriages" recorded in the New Brunswick *Mercury,* 1845-1874. Part 1.

On the Trail of the Pioneers. New England and New York. Office of the Ellen G. White Estate. 1967. 16 pages.

The Pioneers in Historic Michigan. Michigan Conference of SDA. Office of the Ellen G. White Estate. 16 pages.

Whale Fishery of New England. An account, with illustrations and some interesting and amusing anecdotes, of the rise and fall of an industry which made New England famous throughout the world. Printed and published by Reynolds-DeWalt Printing, Inc. New Bedford, Massachusetts. 1968.

INDEX

abolitionist, Bates as 42

Acushnet River, Bates meets neighbor on bridge over 63

Adams, John Quincy, investigates Dartmoor Massacre 26, 27

Advent Herald, attack on Bates in 75

Advent Herald, The, last edition of (1844) 56

Advent Review and Sabbath Herald, first (1850) 73

Advent Shield defends integrity of advent leaders 53

"Adventists" after 1844 61

American Olympiad popular in 1844 57

American Temperance Society, organization and development of 42

American Tract Society, Bates assists in work of 43

Andrews, Charles (prisoner), journal of 25, 26

Andrews, J. N., Bates visits in Iowa 86

Archangel, Russia, Joseph Bates sails for 19

Autobiography, as book, published in 1868 112

   originally published in *Youth's Instructor* 88

Banks of Newfoundland, encounter with icebergs near 19

baptism in Cass River 109

baptism through ice at Monterey, Michigan 87

Bates, Anson, Joseph's older brother, a physician 14

Bates, Anson Augustus, Joseph's first son 31

Bates, Bourne, Sophia, Joseph's older sister 14

Bates, Eliza, Joseph's third child 41

Bates family, health of (1857) 88

Bates, Franklin, Joseph's younger brother, a seaman 14

   takes over *Empress* 38

Bates, Harriot, Joseph's older sister 14

   letter to 111

Bates, Helen, Joseph's second child 31, 32

Bates, Joseph

   birth of 13

   childhood of 15

   schooling (probable) of 16

   going to sea 15, 16

   family tried to dissuade his going to sea 17

   adventure with shark 19

   capture by Danish privateers 20

   impressment into British navy 21

   prisoner of war 21-27

   experiment with drinking 28

   rise from seaman to captain 29, 31

   marriage to Prudence Nye 31

   ships as first mate on *Francis F. Johnson* 31

   description of storm at sea 32

   final voyage on "temperance ship" (1827) 33-39

   conversion 35

   early religious struggles 38, 39

   active in reform movements 41-44

   gives up tea and coffee 44

   joins Millerite movement 46

   vice-president of advent conference 47

   attends first camp meeting 48

   gives fortune to advent movement 49, 50

   sells New Bedford property 50

   reaction to 1844 disappointment 53, 59, 60

   active in promoting Sabbath 60-68

   published tract on Sabbath 61

   visits Wheeler in New Hampshire 63

   meets Ellen White 63

   accepts Ellen White's visions 63

   accident on Erie Canal 64

   travels to "Northwest" 65

   first convert in Michigan 65

   publishes more tracts 66, 67

   financial support for printing 66, 67

   constant traveling 70, 71

   opposes regular publication of Present Truth 73

supports Review and Herald   73, 74
reproved by Ellen G. White   74
contention with Joshua V. Himes
   74-76
makes third visit to Michigan   80
contacts Annie Smith   81
conducts "tent efforts"   82
serves as moderator in meetings for
   organization   84
appeals for literature on ships   85
escapes injury in train accident   85
works in Monterey, Michigan   86
serves as chairman of 1857 conference
   in Battle Creek   87, 89
with J. H. Waggoner in tent meetings
   87
writes autobiography for *Youth's
   Instructor*   88
moves to Michigan   91
chairs various conferences   95, 96
conducts baptism in rainstorm   96
survives first serious illness   96
meets opposition by Cranmer and
   Crozier   97
endures second illness   98
chairs 1860 Battle Creek conference on
   organization   98
contemporaries of, describe his methods
   99
supports James and Ellen White by
   testimonial in *Review*   101
elected first chairman of Michigan
   conference (1861)   101
rebuked by Ellen White for suspicion
   of James White   103
relation of, to health reform   104-107
only leader well during health crisis
   of (1865)   106
reports to *Review* on extensive work
   in Michigan (1865)   107, 108
assigned to organized work in Michigan conference   109
conducts baptism in Cass River   109
visits Governor Crapo   109
second defense of Whites (1869)   114
works on despite wife's death   114
recounts significant dreams   114, 115
held 100 meetings in eleven months
   (1871)   115
describes his health at age 79   115, 116
defends his dietary practices   116

death of   116
Bates, Joseph, Jr., Joseph's fourth child
   41
has accident in whaling   88
death of, at sea   109
Bates, Joseph, Sr., birth and early life
   of   13
wife of   14, 32
will of   14, 32
death of   32
Bates, Mary, Joseph's fifth child   41
Bates, Prudence (Nye), marries Joseph
   31
has letters in *Review*   77, 86
visits New England (1863)   91
death of   114
Battle Creek, first converts in   80
Battle Creek church, cost of   89
Beasley, American consul, fails to secure
   release of American prisoners at
   end of War of 1812   26
"Bloody sixth of April"   27
Boston Tea Party   15
Bourne, Sophia, Joseph's sister, his letter
   to   50
Brooks, Governor of Massachusetts,
   attempts to get Bates released from
   British service   21
Bull Run, Battle of, reaction of Bates to
   101
Butler, George I., opposed organization
   98
Byington, John, elected first General Con-
   ference president   103
rebuked by Ellen White   103

Caledonia, Michigan, Bates chairs conference at   97
camp meeting, at Exeter, New Hampshire
   54, 55
first Millerite, at East Kingston, New
   Hampshire   47, 48
first SDA, at Wright, Michigan   111,
   112
Canada East meeting   47
census, (1820) gives clues on Bates household   32
   (1850) lists members of Bates household   76, 77
   (1860) lists Bates as Adventist minister   98

(1870) reveals facts on Bates family 114

Chester, Maryland, incident in 52

Christian Church, Bates withdraws membership from 49

church, buildings, first, owned by Sabbath-keeping Adventists 83

covenant (not a creed) voted 101

discipline severe at Monterey, Michigan 93, 94

coffee and tea, Bates discards use of 44

Cold Water Army 42

Communist Manifesto initiated in 1844 56

comparison of Joseph Bates with James White 99

conference at Battle Creek in 1860 discusses organization 98

confessions of faith at Monterey, Michigan 94

copyright notice, unusual, in Bates's Sabbath tract 66

Cornell, M. E., baptism of 80

holds effort at Monterey, Michigan 91

works with Bates 83

Couch, Mrs., introduces Samuel S. Snow 55

covenant with God, Joseph Bates's 35

Cranmer (Gilbert), opposes Bates 97

Crapo, Governor of Michigan, Bates visits 109

crisis in 1865 because of health problems 105, 106

Crozier, O. R. L., teaches law done away 97

Danish privateers capture Bates's ship 20

Darden residence, formerly Meadow Farm 16

Dartmore Prison, Bates and other Americans in 22-27

Dartmoor Massacre 26

Dartmouth, the (ship), of New Bedford, in Boston Tea Party 15

defense of Ellen and James White (1869) by Bates 114

denominational statistics at time of 1863 organization 103

diary, Bates's, for 1869 113

"disappointment" of October 22, 1844,

effects of, on believers 58-60

dreams, Bates recounts his 114, 115

Dunn, William (seaman), Captain Bates's troubles with 36-38

Edson, Hiram, writes of 1844 disappointment 58

1844 movement, Bates joins 46

1844, significant events in 56, 57

1845 meeting in Albany, New York 59, 61

Emerson on reform 40, 41

Empress, the "temperance ship" 34-38

epileptic boy healed 80

Fairhaven, Massachusetts, third-ranking whaling center (1831) 14

Fairhaven Academy 15, 16

Fairhaven Antislavery Society, Bates joins 42

Fairhaven Seaman's Friends Society, Bates helps organize 42, 43

Fairhaven Temperance Society, Bates a founder of 41

Fanny (ship), Joseph Bates's first voyage on 18, 19

Farnsworth, Hiram, Bates and Wheeler meet 63

favorite phrases used by Bates 102

final voyage, Joseph Bates's (1827) 33-39

financial help for Bates family, Ellen White appeals for 86

church provides 94

Fitch, Charles, with Hale, presents "43 chart" 47

food supplies at Bates's home (1872) 116

foot washing, early uncertainty on 110

" '43 chart" 47

Francis F. Johnson (ship), Joseph Bates ships as first mate on 31

Garrison, William Lloyd, Bates held high esteem for 43

General Conference (1863) at Battle Creek 102, 103

adopts constitution for General Conference 103

elects John Byington as first president 103

General Conference (1867) discusses foot washing 110
Gibraltar, Bates a prisoner on 21
gift, Joseph Bates's, to the advent movement 49, 50
gold discovered in California 65
Graham, Sylvester, Bates quotes 44
Gurney, H. S., joins Bates in mission to South 50

Hale, Appollos, with Fitch, presents "43 chart" 47
Hall, James Madison Monroe, learns Sabbath truth from Bates 63
hard feelings between Sabbath keepers and other Adventists 75
Harmon, Ellen G. in 1844 58, 60
Harriot, Bates's sister, letter to 111
Hastings, Leonard, Bates's letter to 64
healing by prayer 109
health at age 79, Bates's 115, 116
health problems of leaders cause crisis in 1865 105, 106
health reform, Bates's relationship to 104-107
health reform, early moves toward (1850) 106
health reform, vision of (1863) 106
Hewitt, David, and family, first converts in Battle Creek 80
Himes, Joshua V., publishes *The Signs of the Times* (1840) 46
  Bates's criticism of 74
  criticizes Bates 75
H.M.S. *Rodney*, British warship Bates serves on 21
Hope of Israel, The, tract on Sabbath 62
hymn sung in whalers' chapel 15

Ingraham and Bates rebuked by Ellen White 103
insanity among Monterey church members, reported by Detroit newspapers 92
  denied by *Review* 92
intoxicants prohibited on Bates's ship 37

Jackson, Michigan, work in 65, 66
Jefferson, President, warns of coming trouble over slavery 29

Jessie Dorcas's letter in *Review* 86
Johnny Cake Hill, New Bedford, site of Whaleman's chapel 15

Kellogg, J. P., baptism of 80

Lafayette, Marquis de, recognized Joseph Bates, Sr. 14
Lapeer, Michigan, new church at 95
last by-line, Bates's, in *Review* (November, 1871) 116
Litch, Josiah, works with Himes and Bates 46
Littlejohn, W. H., pastor at Monterey, Michigan 94
  conducted Bates's funeral 94
Littleton camp meeting 48, 49

Madison, President, attempts to gain release of American seamen 21
"mark of the beast," Bates's early teaching on 62, 76
Mary Ann, ship returning American prisoners 27
Mary Armstrong's letter in *Review* on Bates 87
Meadow Farm, childhood home of Joseph Bates 16
Mercury, New Bedford, reports on Dartmoor Prison 27
Michigan, conditions in, before Civil War 79
  first work in 65
  railroads in 79, 80
Michigan Conference, first SDA conference to organize (1861) 101
  first annual session of, 1862, significant actions of 102
  calls on other states to join in 1863 general session 102
Midnight Cry, the, last edition of 56
Miller, William, influence of, on Bates 45, 46
Miller, William, death of 73
mirthfulness decried by 1861 conference 100, 101
mission to Kent Island in Maryland 52
"missionaries," first, to West Coast 111
mixed metaphors in Bates's report 95
Monterey, Michigan, Bates's work in 86, 87

church, details on 91-94
formal organization of (1861) 101
Morgride, Elder Charles, baptizes Joseph
Bates 41
"most honest man in town," Bates in-
quires for 80

New Bedford Academy, description of 16
Joseph Bates, Sr., a founder of 15, 16
Joseph, Jr., probably attended 16
New Bedford, Massachusetts, childhood
home of Bates 13, 14
Nye, Deborah, maiden name of Joseph's
mother 14
Nye, Mrs. Obed, widowed mother of
Prudence, lives in Bates home
31, 32
Nye, Prudence, Joseph Bates marries
28, 31

obituary of Joseph Bates 118
October 22, 1844, Millerites experiences
on 57-59
Ohio, church problems in 80
organization of church, need for recognized 83, 84

Palmer, Dan, (first convert in Michigan)
65
parents, Joseph Bates's, both die (1828)
32
pay for seamen 19
poem read on voyage 34, 35
political situation in 1850 68
Poplar Hill Cemetery, Bates buried in
116
power press for Review, purchase
approved 87
Preble, T. M., publishes tract on Sabbath
62
preparations for Oct. 22, 1844 55-57
press-gang, operation of 20, 21
captures Joseph Bates 21
Princess, British ship Bates assigned to
21
publishing work, designated as Seventh-
day Adventist 100
stabilized by purchase of press 81

Quakers, most New Bedford residents
were 15

Reardon, Mary, Bates's daughter, cares
for aged parents 114
reform movements in America 40-44
real estate transactions of Bates (1830's)
43
religious feelings of Bates during and
after storm 32, 33
resolution of respect for Bates passed by
Michigan Conference 118
Review and Herald, Bates's articles in
82, 107, 116
Bates's letters to 71, 86, 95, 96, 108
109
Revolution, American, Joseph's father
served in 14
Rochester, Massachusetts, Bates's birthplace 13

Sabbath, conferences on 64
Sabbath, hours for observance of 76
Sandwich, Massachusetts, former home of
Joseph's mother 14
second-advent conferences 46, 47
Seventh-day Adventist, Church, nucleus
of (1845-1850) 61
name, approved 98
seventh-day Sabbath teaching rejected by
most Adventists 61, 62
Shannon River, Ireland, crippled ship
enters 19
shark, Joseph Bates's experience with 19
Shortland, Captain, prison governor at
Dartmoor, responsible for massacre
26
Signs of the Times started by Joshua V.
Himes (1840) 46
slavery, Bates's attitude toward 41, 42
Smith, Annie, first contact with Bates 81
wrote poem about early leaders 81
Smith, Gerrit, contact with Bates 71, 73
Smith, Joseph (Mormon), murdered in
1844 56
Smith, Uriah, a convert of Bates 81, 82
secretary at 1860 conference, reports
proceedings for Review 98
Snow, Samuel S., initiates the "midnight
cry" 55
soldiers, returning from Civil War, interest among 109
storm at sea, Bates's description of 32
Stott family living with Bates 76, 77

summary of Bates's contributions 118-120
Sunday observance on Bate's ship 36, 37
Swiftshore, British warship Bates is on when War of 1812 starts 21
swearing prohibited on Bates's ship 36
systematic benevolence adopted 96

table blessing on clean food only 116
"tarrying time" 53, 54
Taylor(President), death of 69, 70
"temperance ship" 37-39
testimony to Bates's health in 1846 by James White 104, 105
tent, description of, used for evangelism in 1850's 87, 88
"tent efforts" by Bates 82, 83
train accident, Bates escapes injury in 85

Van Horn, Bert, former pastor, characterizes Monterey members 92

War of 1812 21, 29
Wareham, Massachusetts, birthplace of Joseph's father 14
Washington, George, President at Bates's birth 13

West, Ellen White urges increased work in 90
Whaleman's chapel 15
whaling industry 14, 15
Wheeler, Frederick, Bates visits 62, 63
White, Ellen G. (Harmon)
    in October, 1844 58
    warns Bates against setting time 60
    meets Bates 63
    accepts Sabbath 63
    reproves Bates 74
    appeals for financial help for Bates 86
    urges increased work in West 90
    visits, and bolsters work in, Monterey, Michigan 91
    Bates supports, with testimonial in *Review* 101
    rebukes John Byington, also Bates and Ingraham 103
    has "health reform" vision 106
    counsels moderation on foot washing question at first 110
    conducts revival at Monterey 111
White, James in 1844 59
Whites at Monterey for meetings 111
Whittier on slavery 70
worship on Bates's ship 37